VIENNA INTERNATIONAL EXHIBITION, 1873.

REPORT

ON

VIENNA BREAD.

BY

E. N. HORSFORD,
MEMBER OF THE SCIENTIFIC COMMISSION OF THE UNITED STATES.

———◆———

WASHINGTON:
GOVERNMENT PRINTING OFFICE.
1875.

TABLE OF CONTENTS.

CHAPTER I.

THE GRAIN OF WHEAT; ITS CHARACTERISTICS.

Art.	Page.
1. The Kaiser-Semmel; characteristics	1
2. Manufacture of Vienna bread	1
3. Scope of the report	2
4. Description of the grain of wheat	2
5. True bran; composition	3
6. Composition of inner layers	3
7. Illustration of structure of bran	3
8. The several coatings of the grain	5
9. Chemical composition of the berry	6
10. Table of analysis	7
11. Distribution of material in the ash	7
12. Phosphoric acid in the ash	7
13. Constituents of the ash	8
14. Proportion of ash	8
15. Source of mineral ingredients of flour	8
16. Proximate chemical ingredients of the berry	8
17. Gluten	8
18. Starch	9
19. Vegetable albumen	9
20. Sugar and dextrine	9
21. Vegetable fibrine and caseine	9
22. Gluten	9
23. Oil	9
24. Cerealine	9
25. Water	9
26. Proximate analysis	9
27. Effect of climate and other influences	10
28. Nitrogenous bodies; their composition	12
29. Sulphates and phosphates	12
30. Gluten; percentage in various flours	12
31. Gluten; its chemical constitution	12
32. Dextrine and its homologues	13
33. Condition of phosphorus in the grain	13
34. Varieties of wheat	13
35. Peculiarities of various flours	14
36. Hungarian wheat	14
37. Nitrogen; its proportion affected by climate	14
38. Climate of Hungary	15
39. Phosphoric acid varies with nitrogen	15
40. Comparison of Victorian with Hungarian wheat	15
41. Redness of color in wheat; its cause	16
42. Hungarian grain; its characteristics	16
43. Table of varieties of Hungarian wheat	16

TABLE OF CONTENTS.

Art.	Page.
44. Kinds of wheat generally sown; its color	18
45. Results of harvesting and grinding Banat and Australian	18
46. European varieties	19
47. Structure of the plant	19
48. Prevention of heating	20
49. Method of thrashing	20
50. American devices used in Austria	20
51. Diseases and enemies of wheat	21
52. Impurities	21
53. Winnowing and separating	22
54. Removal of oats	23
55. Separating light grains	24
56. Separating round seeds	25
57. Another method	25
58. A third device	26
59. Inspection of wheat	27
60. Removal of smut and dirt	27
61. Removal of beard and bran; Bentz's method	28
62. Smut-machines	28
63. Scourer	30
64. Hardiness of Hungarian wheat	30

CHAPTER II.

THE ART OF MILLING.

65. Effect of blows and of pressure on the grain	31
66. Older methods of milling	31
67. Origin of high milling; Vienna grits	31
68. Ignaz Paur; his method	32
69. Paur's apparatus	32
70. Difference between high and low milling	32
71. Jury classification	33
72. High milling; detailed description	33
73. Grades of product	34
74. The characteristic of high milling	34
75. Unpurified grits or middlings	34
76. Finer products of grinding	35
77. Low milling; its product	35
78. Bran	35
79. Constitution and peculiarities of the flour	36
80. Effect of sharpness of cutting edges	36
81. Apparatus required in the process	36
82. Millstones	36
83. Motion of the stone	37
84. Description of the stone	37
85. Arrangement of lands and grooves	37
86. Use of the grooves	38
87. Form used in the United States	39
88. Heating	39
89. Various forms of grooves	40
90. Influence of form and arrangement	40
91. Dimensions adopted	40
92. Brooklyn millstones	40
93. The Thilenius millstone	40

TABLE OF CONTENTS.

Art.	Page.
94. The grain in the mill	41
95. Ventilation	42
96. Cooling	42
97. Cooling indispensable in low milling	42
98. Cylinder-milling; the method	43
99. Illustration of cylinder-milling	42
100. Effect of distance of rolls apart	44
101. Advantages of cylinder-milling	44
102. Wegmann's walzmühle	44
103. The porcelain cylinder-mill	44
104. The St. Gallen mill	46
105. The disintegrator	47
106. Summary	48
107. Sifting or bolting	48
108. The bran-duster	48
109. Proportion of flour attaching to bran	49
110. The flour-bolt	49
111. Purification of grits	50
112. Paur's purifier	50
113. Purifier used at Pesth	51
114. Another device	52
115. Products of the two processes of milling	53
116. Physical differences in wheat	54
117. Advantages of high milling	54
118. Necessity of preserving gluten-cells	55
119. Half-high milling	55
120. Proportion of grades yielded by the two methods	55
121. The low-milling process	55
122. Purification	56
123. Minnesota "Fife" wheat	56
124. Process of milling Fife wheat	56
125. High milling	57
126. Products of Hungarian high milling	57
127. Details of Hungarian milling process	59
128. Grades by numbers	59
129. Comparison by the International Jury	59
130. Flour for Vienna bread	60
131. Grades made at Prague and other mills	60
132. Products of the Prague mill	61
133. Buchholz cylinder-mills	61
134. Average product of the Hungarian mills	63
135. Products of low milling	64
136. A congress of millers desirable	65
137. Advantage of slow reduction	65
138. American methods	66
139. Southern flour	66
140. Impurities in American wheat	67
141. Purification	67
142. Jewell Brothers' practice	67
143. Characteristics of flour	68
144. Varieties of starch-granules	68
145. Structure of the granule	68
146. Characteristics of various starch-granules	69
147. Gluten-cells illustrated	69

Art.	Page.
148. Structure of edible grain	70
149. Effect of milling on the grain	71
150. Hungarian prize-flour	71
151. Its characteristics	71
152. Distribution of nitrogen	72
153. Dempwolff's analysis	73
154. Percentages of products by volumes	73
155. Size of starch-grains and gluten-cells	73
156. Composition of 0 flour and A grits	73
157. Comparison of low and high milled flour	73
158. Nature and cause of grits	74
159. Mode of testing flour	74
160. Aroma of flour	74
161. What causes the dough to "run"	74
162. Chemical examination of flour	75
163. Determination of nitrogenous constituents by specific gravity	75
164. Hungarian mill-industry	75
165. Conclusion	76

CHAPTER III.

MAKING YEAST-BREAD.

166. Signification of the word "bread"	77
167. Leavened and unleavened bread, pastry, and cake	77
168. To secure porosity to the bread	77
169. Fermentation	78
170. The yeast-plant	78
171. Size of yeast-cells	78
172. Blondeau's view of yeast-cells	78
173. Mitscherlich's observations on growth of yeast-plant, with outline diagrams.	79
174. Cavities in yeast-cells	79
175. Effect of heat on cells; effect of solution of sugar	80
176. Cells having cavities convert sugar into alcohol and carbonic acid; character of product dependent on strength of sugar-solution	80
177. Illustration of growth of yeast-plant	81
178. Views of Hassall, Blondeau, Pasteur, and Wiesner	82
179. Theories of fermentation	82
180. What is a ferment	83
181. Different yeast-plants required for different products, according to Pasteur. Liebig's view. Manassein supports Liebig	83
182. Alcoholic fermentation dependent on dynamic condition	83
183. Brefeld's results of research upon alcoholic fermentation	84
184. Effects of fermentation	85
185. Why Hungarian flour will make light bread; why oat, rye, and barley bread is heavy	85
186. Action of lime-water in improving texture of dough	86
187. Problem of a yeast-bread	86
188. The press-yeast of Mautner	86
189. Production of press-yeast from 1846 to 1872	87
190. Preparation of press-yeast	87
191. Several modes of preparation	87
192. Zettler's mode	88
193. Pumpernickel of Westphalia	88
194. Pairs wheat-bread	89

TABLE OF CONTENTS. VII

Art.	Page.
195. Mège Mouriès's method	90
196. Mouriès's grading of products of grinding	90
197. Method of London bakers	90
198. Substitutes for ferment	91
199. Tartaric acid in self-raising flour	91
200. Dauglish's aerated bread	91
201. Phosphatic bread	92
202. Changes of flour in becoming flour	92
203. Changes of starch and gluten	92
204. Changes in crust; conversion of starch to dextrine	93
205. Thickness of crust in large loaves	93
206. Coagulation of vegetable albumen in baking	93
207. Test for phosphoric acid shows it everywhere in crust and crumb	93
208. Advantage of small over large loaves	94
209. Use of steam to prevent formation of thick crust	94
210. Object of keeping bread till it becomes stale	94
211. What is stale bread	95
212. Results of author's experimental research	96
213. Proportions of ingredients in crust and crumb	96
214. Loss of water, as determined by von Fehling	96
215. What is pile?	96
216. Loss due to fermentation	97
217. Question of size of loaf	97

CHAPTER IV.
PROCESSES IN THE VIENNA BAKERIES.

218. Preparation of the roll	98
219. Kaiser-Semmel	98
220. The dough-room	99
221. Preparation of dough	99
222. The oven	100
223. Illustrations of Kaiser-Semmel	100
224. Advantages of Vienna bread	100
225. How to secure large-sized loaves with thin crust	102
226. Advantages to consumer of rolls rather than loaves	102
227. Can we have Vienna bread in America?	103
228. How to make the dough	103
229. Oven and size of loaf	103

APPENDIX A.

230. Dempwolff's investigation of Hungarian wheat and wheat-flour from the Pesth walzmühle	104
231. Products of milling	104
232. Analyses of wheat-flour and ash	105

APPENDIX B.

233. Phosphatic bread	109
234. Author's analysis of prize-flour of Pesth walzmühle	109
235. Liebig's comparison of meats with grain	110
236. Experiments of Magendie and Chossat	110
237. Black bread more nutritious	111
238. Nutritive value of oat-meal porridge and groats; of pumpernickel and rice; of Indian corn, and relations to phosphoric acid	111
239. Phosphates indispensable to vital tissues	111
240, 241. Meyer's experiments with phosphatic bread	111

Art.	Page.
242. Changes produced by fermentation compared with those produced in the phosphatic process	112
243. Advantages of phosphatic bread	112
244. Introduction of phosphatic bread into Europe	113
245. Phosphatic bread made at the Vienna bakery	113
246. Phosphatic bread from Vienna flour	114
247. References	114

ERRATA.

Page 9, line 39: For "hydroscopic" read "hygroscopic."
Page 14, line 31: For "that" read "which."
Page 17, line 1: For "Walzenmühle" read "Walzmühle."
Page 38, line 2: For "lower" read "upper or running."
Page 38, line 3: For "upper or running" read "lower."
Page 38, line 4: For "curves" read "grooves."
Page 44, line 16: For "Walzenmühle" read "Walzmühle."
Page 49, line 16: After "diagrams" insert "from Kick."
Page 86, line 25: For "acetic and" read "acetic or."
Page 86, line 27: For "any" read "in the presence of."
Page 86, line 28: For "so also" read "so is also."
Page 105, line 20: For "ash" read "total wheat;" and over "lime" insert "The total ash contains."

VIENNA BREAD AT THE INTERNATIONAL EXHIBITION.

CHAPTER I.

THE GRAIN OF WHEAT; ITS CHARACTERISTICS.

1. Foreigners visiting the Austrian capital find at every hotel and restaurant the *Kaiser-Semmel*, a smooth, irregularly-rounded, small, wheaten-flour loaf, or roll, of uniform weight, and always fresh, but not warm. It presents a rich, reddish-brown crust, and a delicately-shaded, yellowish, almost white, interior. It is always light, evenly porous, free from acidity in taste or aroma, faintly sweet without addition of saccharine matter to the flour or dough, slightly and pleasantly fragrant, palatable without butter or any form of condiment, and never cloying upon the appetite.

2. This wheat-bread of Vienna has long been famed for its excellence. As produced at the Paris International Exposition in 1867, it elicited universal admiration. The products of the French bakery were, at their best, plainly inferior to the steady, uniform achievements of the Vienna bakery. The proprietors of the latter, when asked what was their secret, replied: "We have none; we use Hungarian flour and press-yeast, and these constituents are manipulated with cleanliness, care and intelligence."

The uniformity of the product demonstrates that the problem of making good bread has been solved. One wonders why such bread cannot be elsewhere obtained. It is known that efforts have been made to introduce the production of the Vienna bread to the public of other countries, but with indifferent success. The trained journeymen-bakers of Vienna are sought for and obtained to serve in other capitals; but the bread they produce is inferior. Why have these efforts failed? Why cannot so apparently simple a process be communicated to others in such terms as to be followed?

To answer this question, the bakers of Vienna determined to give every facility to the visitors at the Exposition to see, if they desired, all the processes essential to the production of their bread. To illustrate the art, they caused a comprehensive bakery, with all needed appliances, to be set up within the grounds of the Exposition, and maintained in full operation from the opening to the close, turning out, day by day, the *Semmel-Brod*, (table-rolls,) loaves of wheat-bread, rye-bread, mixed wheat and rye bread, and numerous forms of biscuit, pastry, cake and confectionery having a basis of flour.

The shelves of the show-room presented the peculiar styles of products to be met with in the different districts of the Austro-Hungarian empire. This extensive bakery was intrusted to the direction of Roman Uhl, of Vienna, court-baker, and the author of various papers on flour, bread and baking.

3. In the study of the processes which, in all their detail, were here laid open to the international jury, as well as to all others interested in the manufactured products of flour, it became apparent that an intelligible report upon the Vienna bread must include a report upon the art of *milling* as practised under the improved methods now pursued in Austria and Hungary, from which latter country the finer Vienna flour is for the most part drawn; and this must be preceded by an account of the structure of the grain of wheat, upon which the philosophy of the improved milling rests. The report must also contain an account of the chemical composition of the grain and flour, and their susceptibilities to climatic influences and to the various agencies of deterioration, and an account of the methods of purification and preservation, upon a knowledge of which the production of the uniformly excellent flour in a large degree depends. It must consider the peculiarities of Hungarian wheat. It must also embrace the history of the improvements in the agencies for rendering the bread porous and free from acid taste or odor, and lastly, present what is essential in the art of baking.

These necessities being recognized, no apology will be required for the attempt to present any details that may enable us to profit by the Vienna exhibition of the art of making bread. They will be confined to the art of making white porous bread from wheat.

4. THE GRAIN OF WHEAT.—The grains or kernels or berries of different varieties of wheat vary from each other slightly in form, but are in general irregularly oblong oval, having a deep groove extending from end to end on one side, which gives to a cross-section a surface bounded by three rounded angles. At one end of the berry is the brush of vegetable hairs; at the opposite extreme, under an irregularly-curved surface-layer of bran technically called the shield, is the embryo. In the accompanying cuts we have, in Fig. 2, at the left, the

Fig. 1. average normal size of the berry, and, in Fig. 1, the same under a power of six diameters, which illustrate the parts referred to.

If the blade of a sharp knife be passed through the berry midway between the two ends and perpendicularly to the axis, there will be presented a section, which, under the microscope, will show an exterior envelope of several layers; an interior envelope, consisting of cells, and their contents of gluten and phosphates, constituting the most nutritious portion of the berry; and a mass of white, consisting of loose cellular

THE GRAIN OF WHEAT.

tissue supporting a vast body of starch-granules, with clusters of cells of albuminoid matter, extending to the heart of the berry. The accompanying diagram,* at the right, which is a cross-section magnified to eighteen diameters exhibits the relative thickness of the outer coats, the gluten and phosphate coat, and the mass of starch and albuminoid cells within, and also the peculiar looped outline of the longitudinal groove on one side of the berry.

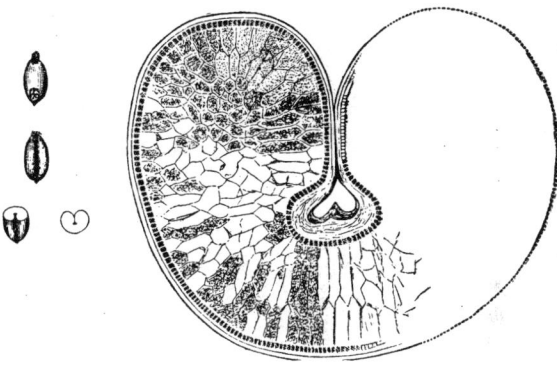

Fig. 2.

5. TRUE BRAN.—If grains of wheat be moistened with water, and rubbed between the folds of a rough cloth, the outer covering may be readily detached. This is composed of two layers, constituting about 3.5 per cent. by weight of the plump unbranned berry. To these layers are attached the vegetable hairs, or beard, at the end of the berry, opposite the embryo. When the dried hulls separated by the rough cloth, are burned, they yield 6.64 per cent. of ash, in which I have recognized, besides the phosphoric acid, notably silicic acid, iron, lime, magnesia, and potassa; of the ash, 7.70 per cent. is phosphoric acid.

6. If the berry, after having been thus hulled, be treated with a solution of alum and then with weak acetic acid, on opening it with a sharp knife along the curved surface on the side opposite the groove, digesting with warm water and subjecting to gentle pressure, the starch and imbedded albuminoid bodies may be quite wholly separated, leaving a layer of cells containing gluten and phosphates, attached to or constituting a part of the inner bran-coat. These inner bran-coats may then with care be successfully freed from the gluten by maceration and gentle pressure. They consist of the honey-combed frame-work of cellular tissue, from which the cells, or sacs, containing the gluten and phosphates have been removed, and the outside layers of envelope not separated with the rough cloth. The weight of these together, including that portion of the outer coats of bran lying within the loop of the groove, shown in Fig. 2, dried at 212° Fahrenheit, is about 12.5 per cent. of the weight of the whole berry. In the ash of all these coats, phosphoric acid, alkaline earths, and alkalies are recognized.

7. In the accompanying diagrams, Fig. 3 illustrates the relative positions of the several layers of the investing coats of the berry, as seen from without; Fig. 4, as viewed in a section transverse to the greater

---

*An absolute portrait, prepared by Mr. Thomas J. Hand, of New York, to whom I am indebted for most of these drawings illustrating the structure of the wheat-grains.

length of the berry; Fig. 5, as presented in longitudinal section. 1, 1 are the outer coats of the bran proper. They are made up of two layers of flattened longitudinal cells. Mégé Mouriès includes both under the name *sarcocarp*, giving to the cuticle or outer wall of the outer layer the name *epicarp*. 2 is the inner coat of bran proper. It is made up of trans-

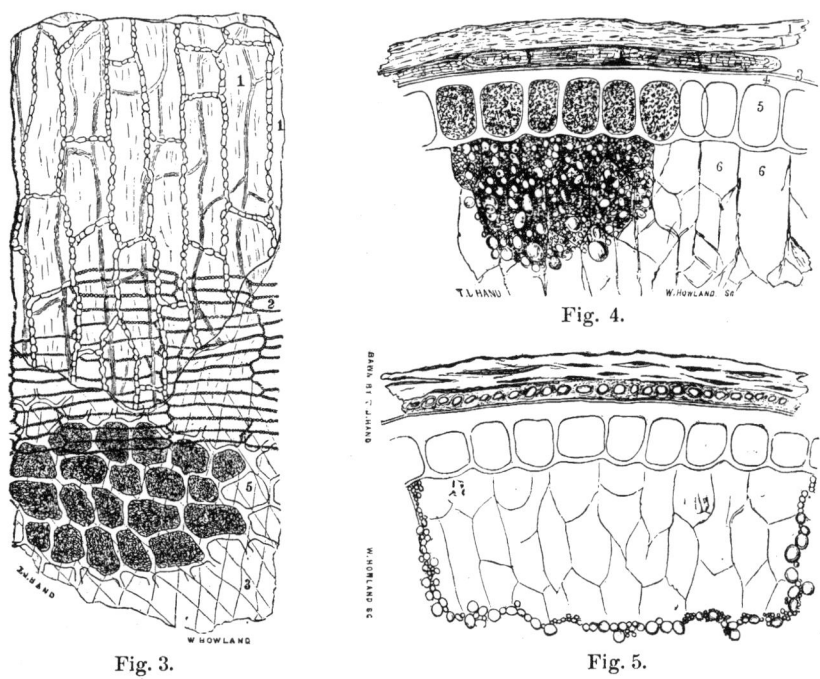

Fig. 3. Fig. 4. Fig. 5.

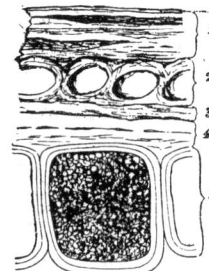

FIG. 6. Portion of radial (or longitudinal) section, 400 diameters.

verse tubes, which, from their arrangement side by side, have suggested the convenient name of *cigar-coat*. The tubes of which this coat is made up have been found by Mr. Hand, in an examination of the residuum of bran after passing through the alimentary canal of a heifer, to be *spiral vessels*. It is the *endocarp*, or fruit-coat of Mégé Mouriès. 1, 1, and 2 together constitute the pericarp of Trécul. 3 is seed-skin, called variously *episperm*, *testa*, and *primine*. In it are the granules of coloring-matter, which determine whether the wheat is red or yellow, or, in their absence, white. 4 is the inner membrane, or *secundine*, the comb-coat, in which are set the gluten-sacs 5, which contain cells holding the gluten and phosphates. 6 is the loose cellular frame-work of the interior, in which are the starch and the imbedded groups of cells containing albuminoid bodies.

Fig. 6.—The gluten-sacs have an average diameter of about $\frac{1}{675}$ of an inch; and the granules of gluten about $\frac{1}{15000}$ of an inch.

The beaded outline of the transverse cells of the cigar-coat, as well as that of the longitudinal cells of the two exterior coats, seems to point to a common structure.

In Fig. 3, the outer coat only was in focus when drawn. The outline of the cells of the inner coat is indicated by shaded lines. Careful microscopic examination shows all these cells to have been tubes, as is indicated in the cigar-coat in Fig. 6.

8. Exposing the whole berry for a few hours to water will cause the outer cells to swell up and appear in cross-section somewhat like, but more flattened than those of the cigar-coat shown in Fig. 6.

Traces of the tubular structure of the longitudinal cells are seen in both Fig. 4 and Fig. 5. One sees, too, not unfrequently, traces of bars across the cells from one bead to its opposite fellow, in a direction slightly oblique to the perpendicular to the axis of the cell. Each bead is seen to be double where two cells lying side by side are seen from above, and a wall of partition is traceable throughout the whole chain. As Mr. Hand has had the fortune to resolve into elastic coils the cells of the cigar-coat, and as it has happened to me to observe them in all perfection in the outer coats of a longitudinal section through the groove and near the embryo, some of them uncoiled in part in the preparation of the section, it seems very possible that these double beads are cross-sections of the two adjacent spiral threads of two adjacent spiral vessels; and that the three coats—that is, the two outer coats of longitudinal cells and the interior cigar-coat of transverse cells, all of which are tubes—were originally so many layers of spiral vessels. The outer cells are flattened, and the traces of the coils of the spiral vessels for the most part obliterated, though the beads which are cross-sections of the double threads, are very distinctly preserved.

According to this view of the structure of the shell of the wheat-grain, the epicarp of Mégé Mouriès is merely the contiguous outer walls of the outer layer of longitudinal spiral vessels, the divisions between the coils of which have been in a large degree obliterated. The sarcocarp, which, with Mégé Mouriès, includes the two coats of longitudinal cells minus the outer wall of the outer coat, (called by him the "epicarp,") should apply only to the inner layer, or mesocarp, and epicarp should apply to the outer layer. Then the cigar-coat will be the *endocarp*. These three belong to the *fruit*-coat, the next two to the *seed*-coat, and all five are exterior to the layer of gluten-sacs and belong to the shell of the grain. Ordinary miller's bran includes these, and carries with them the layer of gluten-sacs in addition, and traces of adhering white flour.

Proceeding from without inward, we should have, as seen in Fig. 7—

Fruit-coats. { 1st. The epicarp, or outer coat of longitudinal cells.
2d. The mesocarp, or inner coat of longitudinal cells.
3d. The endocarp, or coat of transverse cells—the cigar coat.

Seed-coats. { 4th. Episperm, testa, outer seed-coat, or color-coat.
5th. Tegmen, inner seed-coat, or gluten comb-coat, consisting of almost obliterated cells.
6th. Layer of gluten-sacs, or perisperm.
7th. Interior mass of white, consisting of irregular cells containing starch and albuminoid bodies, the endosperm.

Fig. 8.

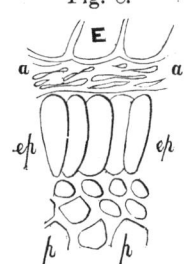

Fig. 7.

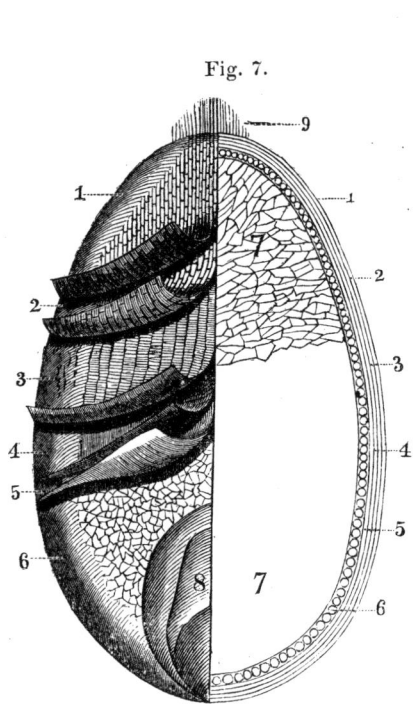

Portion of the epithelium (*ep.*, *ep.*) of the shield, and the neighboring tissues: *p p*, paranchyma of the shield; *a a*, layer of collapsed cells on the border of the endosperm.

Fig. 9.

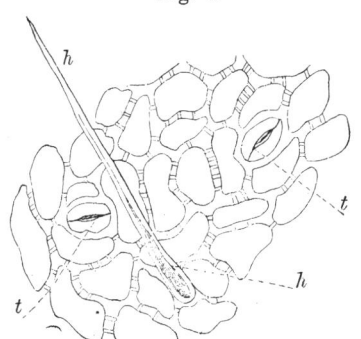

Portion of the outer coat at the end opposite the embryo, with its openings, *t t*, and one of the hairs, *h*, (Vogel.)

At one end, under the shield, 8, are the foreshadowed future plumula and radicle of the embryo. At the other end are the hairs, 9, and occasional openings in the epicarp, as shown in Fig. 9.

Figure 8 presents a greatly magnified section of a minute portion of the tissues of the embryo bordering upon the more interior parts of the kernel.

9. CHEMICAL COMPOSITION OF THE BERRY.—If the kernel of wheat be divided in halves by a sharp blade passing through the grain at right angles to the groove, and one of the surfaces so exposed be subjected to the action of a solution of iodine, it will assume a purple hue, sharply bounded by the gluten-coat, the color of which will be unchanged, showing that the great mass of the interior of the berry is starch. If the other surface be subjected to the action of a solution of blue vitriol

in ammonia (ammonio-sulphate of copper,) the starch of the interior will not be changed in color, but the gluten-coat will have become green from the formation of phosphate of copper. The gluten will also readily absorb red cochineal in solution, while the starch will remain unchanged.

If we take the half of a plump kernel as before, and carefully detach with the point of a needle the starch from the interior, there will remain a cup, the lining of which will be a continuous layer of gluten-sacs set in a comb of cellular tissue, tenaciously binding the sacs together. If this material removed from the interior be burned, the ash remaining will be inconsiderable in amount; but, if the cup be burned, the percentage of ash will be large.

10. A series of fifty-six samples of wheat from various countries gave a percentage of ash from the grains, or berries, dried at 212° Fahrenheit, of from 1.7 to 3.13, with an average of a little less than 2 per cent., almost the whole of which must reside in the 15.5 per cent. of weight of the investing coats of the berry, including the outer and inner bran and the gluten-coat.

The following table may be taken as exhibiting a fair average analysis of the ash of good wheat:

Potassa	30.00
Soda	3.50
Magnesia	11.00
Lime	3.50
Oxide of iron	1.00
Chloride of sodium	0.50
Sulphuric acid	0.50
Silica	3.50
Phosphoric acid	46.50
	100.00

11. The distribution of the materials of this ash is not uniform. The 15.5 per cent. of the investing coats contains much the larger part.

In an analysis of the A grits of the Pesth *Walzmühle* (cylinder or roller mill,) which, as will be seen farther on, may be taken as representing rather more than the average white interior of the berry, exclusive of the gluten-coat, it was found to contain but 0.42 per cent. of ash. Giving to the 3.5 per cent. of outer bran-coats of the total kernel, the ash as found at 6.64 per cent., there would remain, as shown by calculation, for the gluten-coat, a percentage of ash=11.33.

Thus, 3.50 per cent. of 6.64	0.230
And 84 per cent. of 0.42	0.353
There remains for 12.50 per cent. of 11.33	1.417
To make the total ash	2.000

12. The relative proportions of the ingredients of the ash vary somewhat with the physical qualities of the berry.

Ritthausen has found that the hard or flinty varieties of wheat contain an excess of total ash, and in the ash an excess of phosphoric acid as compared with the potassa, and the reverse in soft varieties. In the former, the ash is 2.18 per cent.; in the latter, 1.94 per cent. In the former, the phosphoric acid is to potassa as 51.79 : 33.01; in the latter, as 46.43 : 37.31.

13. The other constituents vary in some sixty analyses that have been compared as follows: Soda, from 0.75 per cent. to 17.79; magnesia, from 7.82 per cent. to 16.27; lime, from 1.07 per cent. to 8.21.

From the researches of Dempwolff it appears that the percentage of lime is greater in the outer coats, while that of the magnesia is greater in the interior portions of the berry. The percentage of potassa is also larger in the interior.

The analyses of the products of the Pesth *Walzmühle* have shown that the phosphoric acid, as will be seen farther on, is in greatly-increased percentage in the investing and gluten coat.

14. The ratio of the ash of the interior to that of the whole grain, weight for weight, would be as 0.42 : 2.00, or nearly as 1 : 5. The ratio of the ash of the interior white portion to the ash of the investing coats, weight for weight, is as 0.42 : 11.33, or nearly as 1 : 27.

15. In view of the above, it is obvious at a glance that, as the interior of the berry contains so little ash, the flour owes its mineral ingredients, when it contains them in considerable proportion, to what it derives from the interior investing coat—the coat containing the sacs of gluten and phosphates. These sacs, detached from the gluten-coat, carry with them the mineral constituents they contain to the flour. It is obvious at a glance, also, that a system of milling is better, generally speaking, in proportion as it contributes from the bran the sacs of this inner coat containing the gluten and phosphates, while leaving behind all that lies outside of this gluten-coat.

16. PROXIMATE CHEMICAL INGREDIENTS OF THE WHEAT BERRY, OR GRAIN.—The investing coats of the berry, including the comb holding the gluten-sacs, consist chiefly of cellular tissue with inorganic salts, mainly phosphates, and small proportions of substances allied to gluten and oil.

17. *Gluten.*—If a handful of flour be moistened and made into dough, and then kneaded in a gentle stream of water until the water runs from the dough clear, the substance that remains when dried is known as gluten, and in its moist condition weighs from 25 to 50 parts of the 100 parts of the flour taken. In its dried condition, it weighs but from 10 to 15 parts. This substance is elastic, tenacious, and possesses the property of absorbing and holding a large percentage of water. When spontaneously dried in the air, it is, chemically speaking, a hydrate, which parts with its water of hydration on the application of heat, which water is re-absorbed from the air on cooling. This property of gluten is of importance, as will be seen farther on in the explanation of

CHEMICAL COMPOSITION OF WHEAT.

the changes fresh bread undergoes in becoming stale, and which take place in the production of toast.

18. *Starch.*—The water that has flowed from the dough in the process of kneading contains, in suspension, the *starch*-granules, and also more or less gluten-cells, which, on standing, settle to the bottom.

19. *Vegetable albumen.*—If the clear liquid above the deposit of starch be poured off and heated to boiling, a foam will appear on the surface, which will collect in the form of gray flakes, strongly resembling coagulated albumen, (white of egg.)

20. *Sugar and dextrine.*—After separating this albuminous substance by filtration, and evaporating the fluid, at a temperature not exceeding 212° Fahrenheit, to the consistency of a sirup, it will be found to be sweet to the taste, showing the presence of *sugar*, (glucose,) and will be found also to contain a body allied very nearly in its properties to *dextrine*, (mucilage.)

21. *Vegetable fibrine and caseine.*—If the crude mass of moist gluten be treated first with weak and then with stronger alcohol, a portion will dissolve, leaving a grayish residue, to which the name of vegetable *fibrine* has been given. The solution in alcohol, on being heated, yields on cooling a deposit of substance having many properties in common with *caseine.*

22. *Glutin.*—If the alcoholic solution be evaporated to the consistency of a sirup, and then water be added, a body of pulpy consistency is separated, which has many properties in common with the albuminoids, already mentioned, but also some properties in common with animal gelatin, justifying a separate name, and it has been called *glutin.*

23. *Oil.*—With the glutin is also separated a fatty body, or oil, of the consistency and melting-point of butter, which may be readily extracted with ether. It is more abundant in the embryo and tissues immediately about it.

24. Besides these nitrogenous compounds, all of which contain phosphates of iron, magnesia, lime, and the alkalies, as well as compounds of sulphur, (sulphates?) another kindred body has been recognized by Mégé Mouriès, which he has called *cerealine*, chiefly found in bran, and which seems to be distinguished from its fellows by greater susceptibility to spontaneous decomposition when moistened and warmed, and a capacity to rapidly liquefy starch. The collective name *aleuron* has been given to all the organized bodies containing nitrogen.

25. To all of these is to be added water in a form that is in part hydroscopic.

26. The proximate analysis of wheat gives us the following constituents: 1. Cellular tissue; 2. Woody fiber; 3. Phosphates, with traces of sulphates, chlorides, and occasionally silicates; 4. Albumen; 5. Fibrin; 6. Caseine; 7. Glutin; 8. Cerealine; 9. Starch; 10. Sugar; 11. Dextrine; 12. Oil; 13. Water.

Oudemans found in 100 parts of wheat-berries—

Starch	57.00
Dextrine	4.50
Nitrogenous substances, soluble in alcohol but insoluble in water	0.42
Coagulable albumen	0.26
Albumen soluble in water and not coagulable, two kinds	1.55
Fibrine	9.27
Oil	1.80
Woody fiber	6.10
Ash	1.70
Extractive matter	1.40
Water	16.00
	100.00

Poggiale found in Egyptian wheat 7.855 per cent. of woody fiber; and, including cellulose and cellular tissue, Polson accredits to a Scotch variety 12.4 per cent.

Alexander Müller found the proportions of component constituents to vary in the wheat-berries grown in the same year and in the same field according as the heavier grains or lighter were taken. Separating the product of pure grain into two parts such that equal volumes weighed in the ratio of 76.75 : 52.55, he obtained from 100 parts of each—

Water	15.65	15.56
Woody fiber	2.54	6.04
Ash	1.57	1.80
Nitrogenous substance	11.84	12.97
Oil	2.61	2.39
Sugar	1.41	2.40
Starch	64.38	58.84

From the above, it is apparent that the heavier grain contains more starch, but less of nitrogenous substance, sugar, and woody fiber.

27. To the above may be added a table embracing results showing how greatly the composition of the wheat-berry is influenced by differences in season, soil, climate and variety:

CHEMICAL COMPOSITION OF WHEAT.

Authorities.	Names of varieties.	Water.	Starch.	Fat.	Cellulose, (woody fiber, cellular tissue.)	Gum and sugar.	Nitrogenous substances.	Nitrogen.	Ash.	P O₅.	Si O₂.
Falling & Faiset*	Winter-wheat, (Würtemberg)	14.78	31.95		2.84		13.24		1.97	0.71	0.14
Millon†	Twenty-two samples from Lisle, Algeria, and Odessa.	12.01–17.70		1.41–2.14	1.40–2.35		9.92–13.81	1.59–2.73			
Polson ‡	Old American	10.8	62.3	1.2	8.3	3.8	10.9		1.6		
	New Scotch	14.8	56.9	1.2	12.4	5.3	7.0		1.5		
Poggiale §	Mean of samples not specified	14.5	63.3	1.9	4.2		17.4		1.7		
Mayer ‖	Summer-wheat	13.47						2.29	2.19	1.18	
	Winter-wheat, nine samples	10.97–13.83						2.01–2.32	1.89–2.36	0.93–1.16	
Horsford ¶	Talavera wheat	15.43					13.98	2.59	2.80		
	Whittington wheat	13.93					14.72	2.68	3.13		
	Sandomiertz wheat	15.48					14.51	2.69	2.40		

* Dingler's Polytechnisches Journal, cxxiv. The moisture was determined in the fresh grain. The other constituents in the grain were dried at 212° Fah.
† Compt. Rend., xxxviii. Amount of dry gluten in the nitrogenous substance varied from 6.0 to 7.04. (?)
‡ Chem. Gaz., 1855, p. 211. The determinations refer to the grain in its ordinary (undried) state.
§ J. Pharm., (3), xxx, 180, 25. The determinations refer to the substance dried at 248° Fah. The water was determined by heating to the same temperature. The starch includes gum or dextrine.
‖ Liebig's Annalen, ci, 129. The water was determined in the air-dried grain; the other materials in the grain dried at 212° Fah.
¶ Liebig's Annalen, 1846. The nitrogenous substance was calculated from the percentage of nitrogen in the air-dried condition.

28. NITROGENOUS BODIES.—The organic elements of the several nitrogenous bodies in the foregoing tables are not only the same, but are substantially in the same proportions. The average analyses yield—

Carbon 53.5
Hydrogen 7.0
Nitrogen 16.0
Oxygen, phosphates and sulphates 23.5

100.0

29. The sulphates and phosphates vary in quantity and proportion much from each other, and are doubtless connected with the chemical and physical qualities of the different nitrogenous substances of which they constitute a part.

30. GLUTEN may be estimated either moist or dry, as already pointed out. The average of nine varieties from different countries in Europe, determined long since by Vauquelin, gave for the moist gluten 25.57 per cent. of the flour, and for the dried 10.69 per cent.

The determinations of the percentage of moist gluten in the flour from certain varieties of wheat exhibited at the International Exhibition of 1873, made by Franz Schmidt of Langendorf near Vienna, a member of the international jury, gave the following results:

Varieties of wheat-flour: *Percentage of moist gluten in the flour.*

Flour, by the process of high milling, from the Vienna Fruit and Flour Exchange 37.5
Flour, by the process of low milling, from the German Collective Exhibition 25.5
Extract flour, from Economo, in Trieste 44.25
Flour of the Hungarian Collective Exhibition 37.0
Flour from Banadura wheat from Russia, by A. Bakhrameiff ... 48.65
Flour from Liaschkoff, (from white wheat) 35.3
Flour of G. C. Thilenius, Cape Girardeau, Missouri, (from American white wheat) 32.5
Flour from the hard wheat of Algiers 32.5
Italian flour from Besareth in Ancona 25.0
Spanish flour 30.0
Japanese flour 37.5

31. Von Bibra analyzed the gluten obtained from several varieties of flour, and found the proportions of vegetable fibrine, gelatine, and caseine to be as shown in the accompanying table:

Ingredients.	Imperial flour, finest numbers.				Medium flour.		Fine Spelz flour.			Three varieties of wheat-flour.		
	1	2	3	4	1	2	1	2	3			
Vegetable fibrine	7.95	71.55	69.40	70.48	81.61	78.62	70.22	71.14	71.90	71.29	70.73	71.20
Vegetable gelatine	14.40	16.00	17.57	16.92	7.54	8.35	16.53	15.36	17.20	19.56	13.64	15.43
Vegetable caseine	8.80	6.53	7.30	6.33	3.85	4.88	7.08	7.20	6.29	4.01	9.35	7.40
Oil	5.83	5.92	5.73	6.27	7.00	8.15	6.17	6.24	4.61	5.14	6.28	5.97

32. DEXTRINE, WOODY FIBER, CELLULOSE, STARCH, AND GLUCOSE.—
The composition of starch, dextrine, woody fiber and cellular tissue
shows the carbon, hydrogen and oxygen to be in the same equivalent
proportions, and are given in the formula—
$$C_{12} H_{10} O_{10}$$
Glucose (fruit sugar) contains two atoms more of water, and has the
formula—
$$C_{12} H_{12} O_{12}$$
This is the body into which starch and dextrine are converted by the
action of ferment; and, by a kindred reaction, the glucose is converted
into alcohol and carbonic acid, as given in the following equation :
Glucose. Alcohol. Carbonic acid.
$$C_{12} H_{12} O_{12} = 2 (C_4 H_6 O_2) + 2 (C O_2)$$
These changes, which play so important a part in giving porosity to
bread by the yeast or leaven process, will be considered farther on.

33. That the phosphorus of wheat is present in the form of phosphoric acid, is evident from the experiments already mentioned, of treating the cross-section of wheat with ammonio-sulphate of copper, which yields a green substance, phosphate of copper, and flour with a solution of ammonio-nitrate of silver, yielding a yellow body, the tribasic phosphate of silver.

The circumstance that phosphoretted hydrogen is set free in the putrefactive fermentation of dough does not antagonize this conclusion, since superphosphate of lime composted with fermenting organic matter will yield the same product.

That the sulphur of the gluten and kindred bodies is in the form of sulphuric acid or sulphates, is exceedingly probable, though it is difficult to determine this point, because it is not easy to disengage the sulphuric acid without subjecting the flour to processes which involve the hazard of oxidation.

The circumstance that sulphuretted hydrogen is evolved in the process of putrefactive fermentation of moistened flour is not opposed to this conviction, since sulphates are readily reduced by liquid organic matter; as, for example, the action of ether upon sulphate of lime, which after a time yields the odor of sulphuretted hydrogen.

34. VARIETIES OF WHEAT.—The genus *Triticum* includes two species, *T. vulgare* and *T. spelta* and a vast number of varieties. These varieties differ from each other, whether bearded or not, whether single-headed or many-headed, whether having white or red chaff, and whether of white or red berry, or bluish; they differ in their period of ripening, in susceptibility to climatic influences, and in yield.

The general structure of the grain, physically considered, varies somewhat; and the composition as revealed by proximate and ultimate analysis also varies. There is a plump and a slightly shrunken berry; a brittle and a tough berry; a berry containing more lime and magnesia and one containing less of these ingredients; a berry in which the soda which is usually present in small quantity is very greatly increased

The gluten, the starch, the several nitrogenous substances, and the phosphates vary in proportion to each other and to the whole.

35. There is one quality in which samples of wheat differ very greatly from each other. It is in the products yielded by the grain when subjected to pressure or a blow, as in the process of converting it into flour. In this, the grains of different districts and of the same district in different years vary greatly. The Hungarian varieties selected for the production of the choicest flour and bread at Vienna were distinguished in these latter peculiarities. They yielded a more *gritty* flour.

36. HUNGARIAN WHEAT.—It would be perhaps difficult to determine to what special agency the marked superiority of the Hungarian wheat, or perhaps it should be said of the Hungarian flour, is to be ascribed; but, aside from the constant care of the farmer in changing the varieties grown, with the slightest deterioration in quality of the products, it is believed to be due largely to the *dryness and clearness of the atmosphere of the region in which the wheat is grown, at the time when the contents of the berry are in the condition technically known as " milk."*

37. "The climate of the Hungarian lower lands is marked by frequent and extreme vicissitudes. It is a continental climate. The modifying influence of the sea is not appreciable." As a consequence of the dryness of the air, notwithstanding the tolerably cool nights, there is no dew in summer. Soon after sunrise, the temperature rises to 74°–77° Fahrenheit, and in the course of the day attains from 95° to 100°, and there remains until nearly sunset. Not infrequently, the rain-storms, commencing in violence, pass over to a mild continuous rain, which seldom lasts more than two days, and produces an astonishing development of vegetation.

The driest months are July and August. Taking the average yearly moisture in the air in the mountain-lands at 81°.5, (maximum 100°,) in the west and southwest portions of Hungary it is 76°.5 and in the plains 71°, that is 8° lower than prevails in the North German plains.

The total annual rain-fall in all Hungary is 24 inches, distributed through 107 days. In the plains, it sinks to 19 inches, and this falls in 96 days.

The average mean annual temperature of Pesth is 51°.88.* The Hungarian summer is uniformly very dry.

38. How is this dryness to increase the percentage of nitrogen? The explanation would seem to be found in the more rapid evaporation of water from the leaves, which brings up the water from the soil and with it whatever is held in solution.

It would be expected that the inorganic constituents which are in solution in the water should be in augmented percentage; and this has been found to be the case. Mayer found the phosphoric acid to increase with the nitrogen, and believed the production of nitrogenous bodies depend-

---

*From the "*Skizze der Landskunde Ungarns*," prepared as an introduction to the catalogues of the Hungarian department at the Vienna Exposition.

EFFECT OF CLIMATE ON WHEAT. 15

ent on the presence of the phosphates. He found the ratio of phosphoric acid to wheat in the dried kernels to be as 1.078 : 2.20, or 100 parts of phosphoric acid to 204 parts of nitrogen. Ritthausen found the proportion of nitrogen somewhat higher, 100 of phosphoric acid to 258 of nitrogen.

39. The effect of the Hungarian climate on the development of the white wheat of Australia brought into Hungary and cultivated there, is seen on comparing sections of the original Victoria wheat with the product of the same grain after some time growing in Hungary in several particulars : 1. The kernels, which were originally white, have changed more or less perfectly to red; 2. In some, the portions most remote from the outer shell are still white or clouded ; 3. In others, the whole of the kernel on one side of the groove is red, and a patch of the other from the surface inward remains white ; 4. On shaving thin slices from a transverse section of such a kernel, the white part is found to be relatively tenacious, while the red is brittle; 5. In thin slices, the red portion appears quite as white as the white portion. It is perhaps safe to say that the Hungarian red berries are, as a general rule, more shriveled, more angular, or less rounded, than the white kernels of Victoria. They certainly are more shriveled than the samples of what is known as plump wheat in the United States.

40. RELATION OF CLIMATE TO THE PERCENTAGE OF NITROGEN.—Laskowsky investigated a large number of Russian varieties of wheat collected at the great Russian Agricultural Exposition in 1864, determining their percentages of water, nitrogen, and oil. He found that, as compared with the wheat of other countries, especially those to the west of Russia and nearer to the sea, the Russian wheat was richer in nitrogen. The climate of Russia in the same latitudes was colder in winter, and warmer and drier in summer. The farther east one goes, the warmer does he find the summer, and the less the rain-fall. If this be the cause of the greater percentage of nitrogen, it ought to be found that, as one recedes from the sea-coast, the percentage of nitrogen in the wheat should increase ; and, as a matter of fact, this is the case, as the following table, taken from Kerl & Stohlman's Technische Chemie, will show :

Percentage of nitrogen.
Scotland, (v. Bibra).. 2. 01
North and Middle France, (Reisch)............................ 2. 08
Neighborhood of Lille, (Millon)................................. 2. 18
Chemnitz, Saxony, (Siegert)....................................... 2. 42
Bavaria, (Mayer)... 2. 20
Eldena, Baltic Sea, (v. Bibra).................................... 2. 18
Raitz Blansko, Mähren, (Gohren)................................ 2. 36
Poland, (Peligot)... 2. 68
Odessa, (Millon).. 3. 12
Toganrog, (Peligot)... 2. 54
Rjasan, (v. Bibra)... 2. 47

	Percentage of nitrogen.
Samaria, (v. Bibra)	3.47
European Russia, (Laskowsky)	3.58
Government of Wilna	1.95
Eriwan, (between Caspian and Black Seas)	4.30
Central Russian governments	3.37
South and Southeast Russian governments	3.72
Siberia, (v. Bibra)	2.65
Tobolsk, (Laskowsky)	2.74

41. To what the redness of red wheat is due may be seen under the microscope.

The hyaline coat—the testa—immediately within the cigar-coat, like the *rete mucosum*, is the seat of the pigment. In unripe grain, it may be seen to contain fine yellowish or brownish-red granules. Where both are wanting, and the interior is mealy, the berry is white. Where the granules are yellowish, the berry corresponds in color. Where the berry is red, the granules of the testa are red.

It has been stated to me by an experienced miller that in some samples of wheat the red matter of the interior of the groove is so abundant that it is quite impossible to obtain from them a white flour. It is spoken of by some millers as having a gummy consistency. I have carefully compared a very large number of analyses, organic and inorganic, proximate and absolute, to see if there exists any constant quantitative inorganic concomitant of the redness or whiteness of wheat. It is probably, purely organic. Mr. Thomas J. Hand, in his paper on "Wheat: its Worth and Waste," states that in the fully ripe wheat he examined, the cell-structure of the coloring matter was no longer defined. The coat was too delicate and filmy to be justly represented in a sectional view.

What agency determines whether a wheat-berry shall be red or white—that is, whether the color-coat shall be red or otherwise—is not clear. It is unquestionably a quality in part due to the original variety, and in part to conditions of growth at particular stages of progress toward maturity.

42. The berry from which the best Hungarian flour is made, is for the most part, of reddish color, is slightly shrunken, and cuts with a sharp knife throughout the cross-section something like the rind of old cheese. Under a sharp blow, it cracks into lumps. It reminds one of our best so-called southern wheat.

The plump, full berry, so abundant in the collections of the Northern Pacific Railroad, from the valleys of the Saskatchewan, in the American department of the Exposition, when laid open with the knife, presents a relatively less flinty or hard interior; the investing coats only of the wheat presenting any considerable obstruction to the edge of the blade. Under a sharp blow it readily falls to powder. It is uniformly larger than the Hungarian berry.

43. Through the kindness of Graf Heinrich Zichy, of Oedenburg, Hungary, president of the international food-jury, and under the immediate

superintendence of Herr Dosswald, director of the Pesth *Walzenmühle*, a collection of all the choice varieties of wheat grown in Hungary, and of those grown with success in some other countries and introduced into Hungary, has been supplied to aid in this investigation. The list includes in all 42 samples.

44. VARIETIES OF WHEAT WHICH ARE PRODUCED IN HUNGARY.—

GROUP I.

1. Békés improved Hungarian wheat.
2. Scönyer Hungarian wheat from poorly-tilled soil.
3. Scönyer Australian wheat from well-tilled soil.
4. Tolnan wheat.
5. Temeser Comitat Hódoser wheat grown in stubble-field.
6. Banat Hódoser wheat grown after corn.
7. Banat Hódoser wheat grown in fallow field.
8. Erczier wheat.
9. Erczier wheat of 1874.
10. Autumn-wheat from Upper Hungary south of the Danube.
11. English wheat from the Banat.
12. Neograde wheat.
13. Theis wheat.
14. Theis wheat improved.
15. Veszpremer Comitat Adelaide wheat.
16. Veszpremer Comitat Theis wheat.
17. Australian Victoria wheat, Borsodor Comitat, 1873.
18. Victoria wheat, 1874.

GROUP II.

19. Summer or winter wheat with white heads.
20. Improved Caucasian wheat.
21. Triticum amylon album.
22. Triticum compactum nudum rubrum.
23. Triticum vulgare nudum.
24. Triticum vulgare Littorale Hungaricum.
25. Triticum vulgare nigro aristatum Banaténse.
26. Blè Mars. Triticum nudum æstivum.
27. Triticum album densum.
28. Triticum turgidum spica, aristis violaceis.
29. Triticum Hungaricum rubrum nudum.
30. Triticum vulgare aristatum rubrum.
31. Triticum durum aristatum rubrum.
32. Triticum vulgare albo aristatum.

GROUP III.

33. Neograde wheat.
34. Theis wheat.

35. Yellow Banat wheat, Lower Banat.
36. Red Banat wheat, Banat.
37. Weissenburg wheat.
38. Pest-soil wheat.
39. Wheat from the Upper Hungary plateau.
40. Original Adelaide wheat.
41. Hungarian wheat from Australian seed.
42. Slovak wheat.

Extract from the report transmitted by Graf Zichy.—"In the first place, winter and summer wheat succeed. Both may be bearded or bald; all are cultivated.

"Some varieties have short berries, and others are long with corresponding diameters.

"The color is sometimes dark and sometimes light. The dark color is found among all native varieties; the light is found in all imported varieties.

"As a general thing, Banat wheat is sown. In all parts of the kingdom, occasionally, changes in the seed yielding other formed and colored berries of Banat wheat appear, as a consequence solely of degeneration.

"Besides the Banat wheat, in recent times there have been sown Australian and Victoria wheat with some success."

45. "Here follow the results of harvesting and grinding of samples of these two kinds:

"FIELD-PRODUCTION.

"Banat wheat, 19 metzen* per 1,600 □ °.†
"Australian (Adelaide) wheat, 25 metzen per 1,600 □ °.

"MILLING-RESULTS.

"*Banat wheat.*

	Per cent.	
"Flour, No. 0–2	14.1	} 19.4
"Flour, No. 3	5.3	
"Flour, No. 4	8.2	} 24.7
"Flour, No. 5	16.5	
"Flour, No. 6	13.2	} 21.4
"Flour, No. 7	8.2	
"Flour, No. 8	7.6	
"Bran, No. 9	17.6	
"Bran, No. 10	3.0	
"Waste, No. 11	2.3	
"Loss	4.0	
	100.0	

* Metzen = 16.2 wine-gallons.   †□° = unit of land-measure.

VARIETIES OF WHEAT. 19

"*Australian wheat.*

	Per cent.	
"Flour, No. 0*	4.7	} 23.8
"Flour, No. 3	19.1	
"Flour, No. 5	24.0	
"Flour, No. 6	27.3	
"Flour, No. 8	2.5	
"Bran, No. 9	12.0	
"Bran, No. 10	6.0	
"Loss	4.4	
	100.0	

"GLUTEN, (MOIST.)

"*Banat wheat.*		"*Australian wheat.*	
	Per cent.		Per cent.
"No. 0	36	"No. 0	32
"No. 3	37	"No. 3	35
"No. 5	38	"No. 5	45
"No. 6	46	"No. 6	40
"No. 8	26	"No. 8	47

"The experiments of the bakery show the superiority of the Hungarian wheat. On the whole, the Australian wheat soon degenerates and becomes inferior to the Banat wheat.

"Altenburg, Hungary.

"GRAF RENNER."

46. The varieties of wheat recognized in the botanical gardens and agricultural institutions of the different states of Europe are numerous. Before me is a list of forty varieties prepared in Saxony. The number produced at Hohenheim, in Würtemberg, is large. Most of these, and doubtless many others, were on exhibition at the Exposition, in many instances exquisitely arranged.

In the pavilion of Prince Schwarzenberg, effect was added to the display by arranging the different varieties in contiguous variously-shaped cells constituting a mosaic, in which the different shades of color and the varieties in form were brought into contrast. The collections of the different states of the German empire were most extensive, as were also those of the Austro-Hungarian empire, and indeed of most of the countries represented at the Exposition.

The collection sent by the direction of the Northern Pacific Railroad was of great excellence, variety, and extent, and received the medal of *merit.*

47. STRUCTURE OF THE WHEAT-PLANT.—In the agricultural collections of Germany and Austria particularly, there were most carefully

---
*The terminology of the Hungarian milling-system—the meaning of the numbers—will be presented under the subject of milling.

prepared specimens illustrating the structure of the whole plant; its growth, and especially the influence of the condition of the subsoil upon the development of the fibers of the roots. These were presented in their whole length and utmost detail, exhibiting in some instances an extension from the surface of the soil downward exceeding a full yard.

The specimens prepared by Baron Horsky, of Horskysfeld, near Kolin in Bohemia, attracted special attention, as showing how far, where the soil is penetrable, the roots will extend to reach water or needed nutriment.

48. THE PRESERVATION OF WHEAT IN LARGE MASSES AGAINST HEATING.—The excellence of the Vienna bread is not due to any single peculiarity in the processes pursued by the Vienna baker, but is to be ascribed to the fidelity with which the susceptibilities of the grain are respected and observed in all the changes to which it is subjected, from the time the seed-wheat is selected and sown, through all the career of growth and ripening, the harvesting and the threshing, transportation, keeping in the granary, and milling, to the time when the selected portions are subjected to the processes of the baker resulting in bread.

The moist atmosphere which characterizes the English climate, and so frequently interferes with the harvesting there, and not infrequently does great injury to the crops in some sections of our own country, both before and after the grain is cut, and previous to its being stacked or housed or threshed, is unknown in Hungary. Great care is taken, in the erection of the shocks in the field, to allow any rain that may fall to run readily off or speedily to dry away. Few things impress the traveler, in passing through the Austrian empire at the conclusion of the wheat-harvest, with more grateful surprise than the carefully constructed and capped shocks of moderate uniform size and almost military regularity of arrangement, in which the wheat remains in the field to become thoroughly dried, preparatory to the gathering into stacks or barns to be threshed.

49. In threshing the grain, the flail is still extensively used in various parts of Austro-Hungary.

Care is taken, when the grain has been threshed, cleaned, and prepared for market, and when the quantity is small and not thoroughly dry, by occasional turning over with the shovel, to expose all parts of it repeatedly to the air, and so prevent "heating," and to destroy any microscopic vegetation or mold, the spores of which are ready to take advantage of the moist surface of the berry and work the deterioration of its contents.

50. On the estate of Baron Horsky in Bohemia, which was exhibited to the food-jury, was a so-called American granary, provided with an elevator for the purpose of carrying the grain to the uppermost of a series of perforated floors or shelves, by means of which the grain could be made to fall in numerous slender streams through successive air-

spaces to the hopper at the bottom, from which the grain was again carried in the buckets of the elevator to be discharged on the upper shelf, and so made to go round and round until the desired dryness had been obtained. This is only one of the numerous devices which this prince of agriculturists has introduced for the scientific solution of the problem of producing a perfect wheat-berry. An apparatus for this purpose, to be used also as a malt-kiln and malt-sprouter, by Joseph Geeman, of New York, exhibited in the American department of the Exposition, received the distinction of honorable mention.

51. DISEASES AND ENEMIES OF THE WHEAT.—Among the most interesting of the exhibitions of material for illustration in the department of technical education, from Bohemia, Hungary, Austria, and the German empire, were elaborate preparations of the various insect-enemies, presenting their habits, the development of their eggs in all stages of their growth, and the modes by which the injuries effected by them are accomplished.

It is to be regretted that it is quite impossible to give any description commensurate with the merit of this department of the Exhibition, as in many cases they existed only in the particular samples submitted at the Exposition, and were accompanied by no special description.

These results of the labors of love on the part of teachers and of institutions for instruction in technical education were eminently suggestive to any one interested in object-teaching, and showed how possible it is to bring within the sphere of thorough scientific investigation the minutest conditions upon which the success of the practical agriculturist depends.

Wheat-blight, rust, ergot, honey-dew, Hessian fly, and the red, black, and white weevil are familiar names; but how much more would they signify to us with scientifically-arranged actual specimens, displaying the results of anatomical dissection and microscopic analysis, illustrating every stage of their growth and their habits, the parts of plants in which the eggs and spores are deposited, and the kind and extent of injury which they produce!

52. IMPURITIES IN WHEAT.—Commercial wheat is rarely absolutely pure. Beside the dust and sand, chaff and straw, there are numerous seeds which more or less find their way through the fanning-mill to the granary, and require to be separated from the wheat-berry before the wheat is fit for grinding. Among these may be mentioned numerous varieties of wild onions, vetches, pease, parsley, beans, radishes, mustard, chess, oats, grass-seed, cockle, fragments of straw and chaff, &c. All these, together with blasted kernels of wheat, rust, and ergot, (smut,) must be effectually removed.

It is plain that shriveled or blasted berries in the process of milling would, for the most part, be resolved into fine bran, and so be with difficulty separated from the flour, and thus the flour discolored and rendered less nutritious.

Some of the foreign seeds impart unpleasant taste; some are not wholesome for food; and most of them impair the color of the flour.

53. Various mechanical devices are in use for separating the light grains from the heavy, and the foreign seeds, grains, and other impurities from the sound wheat. The sieve is one; another is the blower, causing a current of air to act upon a thin cascade of falling grain.

In the sifting process, advantage is taken of the unequal size and of the different shapes of the bodies to be separated from each other. It is easy to see how light grains and chaff, bits of straw and fine dust, would be farther diverted from a perpendicular in falling through a current of air driven by a revolving fan than the heavy sound grain. This principle was illustrated in the earliest times when the mixed wheat and chaff were tossed together into the air to be separated by the wind before reaching the ground, and is the principle underlying the ordinary fanning-mill.

The separation of mustard, cockle, and grass seed from the wheat may be easily effected by passing the mixed grains over inclined plates perforated with holes large enough for the smaller seeds to pass through but not large enough for the wheat.

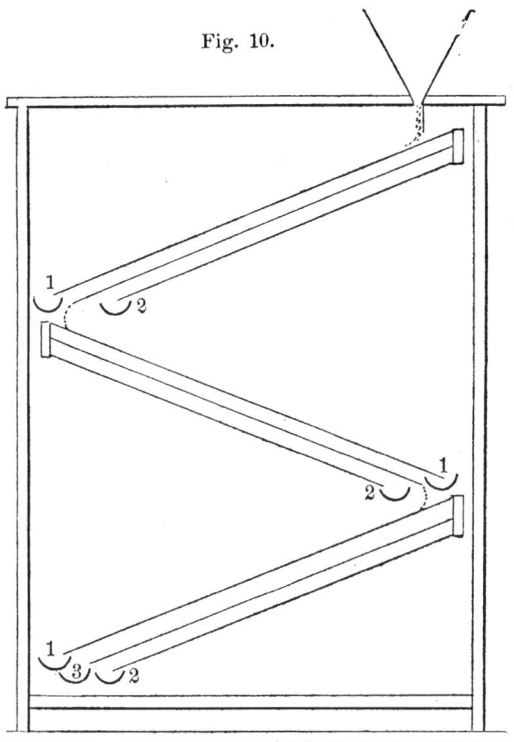

Fig. 10.

Sketch of side view of Jewell's separator.
1, oats, chaff, &c.
2, mustard, cockle, grass-seeds, &c.
3, sound wheat.

APPARATUS FOR PURIFYING WHEAT. 23

54. The oat-grain is separated by taking advantage of its elongated form. The mixed oat and wheat grains are discharged in a thin sheet upon an inclined jogging, thin iron plate, perforated with round holes, at intervals nicely determined by experiment, abundantly large for the ready passage of both the wheat and oat grains if presented end foremost perpendicularly to the surface of the plate. But as the plate is inclined, each berry must be tipped forward in order to enter a hole. An individual hole is of such diameter that when the wheat-grain sliding forward carries its center of gravity beyond the support of the upper edge of the hole, there will be room for the prow, that is, the forward end of the grain, to sweep downward through the hole without striking its lower margin, and thus the wheat-grain be separated. The oat-grain, however, in sliding down the inclined plane, before the center of gravity has passed beyond the support of the upper margin of the hole,

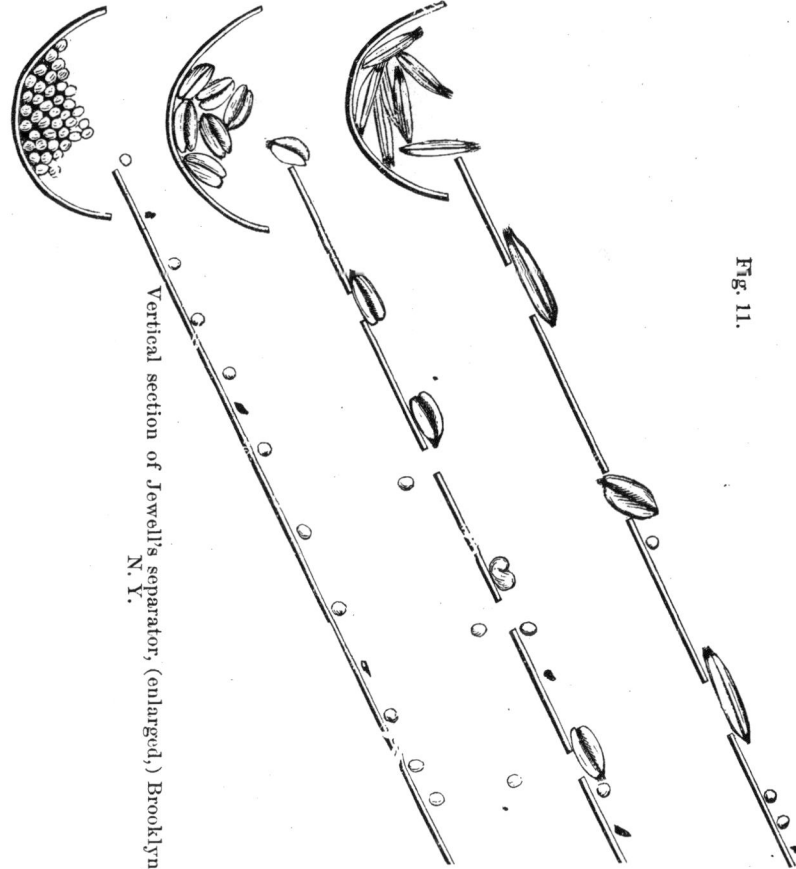

Fig. 11.

Vertical section of Jewell's separator, (enlarged,) Brooklyn, N. Y.

will, by reason of its prolonged hull, extend over the lower margin of the hole, and thus fail to fall through. As the oat-grain advances, the center of gravity will pass beyond the lower edge of the hole and gain the support of the continuous surface before the tail of the berry will have lost the support of the upper edge. The accompanying cuts (Figs. 10 and 11) illustrate without further explanation the process by which the

Fig. 12.

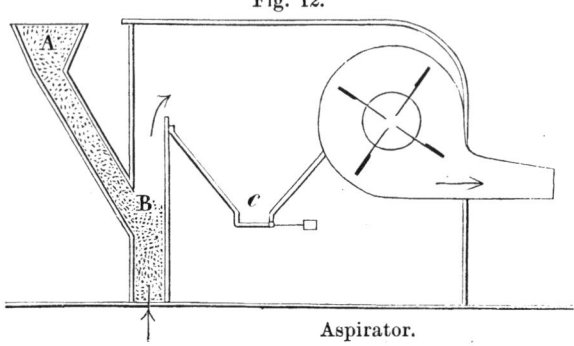

Aspirator.

oat-grains are separated from the wheat. Fragments of straw and chaff will pass on with the oat; while mustard and other seeds smaller than the wheat are separated by a second screen.

Fig. 13.

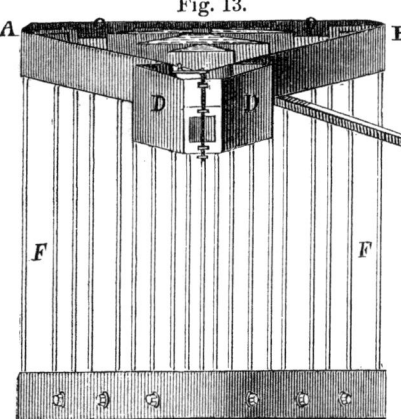

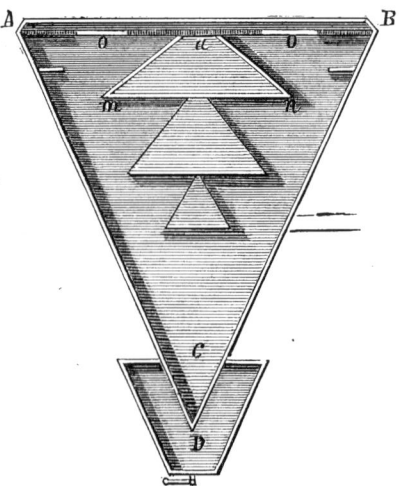

Hignette's stone-separator.

55. For the separation of the heavy or sound from the light or blasted kernels and from straw or chaff, the apparatus shown in Fig. 12, and called an aspirator, is employed. The wheat enters at A. The current of air enters through the falling grain at B, drawn by the exhaust-fan. The heavier kernels drop directly down. The lighter and blasted kernels fall to C, and the lighter chaff and straw pass out through the exhaust-chamber.

This apparatus was on exhibition as Bauer's patent exhaust-purifier or aspirator.

To separate the heavy from the light grains, and also to separate coarse sand or minute pebbles from wheat, the machine shown in Fig. 13, and known as J. Hignette's stone-separator, was on exhibition.

The grain enters at A from a spout, upon a slightly inclined surface, resting on slender wooden supports. As a consequence of a peculiar jarring or shaking, the heavier particles or grains work toward the angle C, where they drop into the compartment D, while the lighter escape over the low passes at o o'.

56. SEPARATING ROUND SEEDS.—Another device has been employed in the neighborhood of Vienna, in which advantage has been taken of the spherical form of certain of the foreign seeds to effect their removal.

The wheat, with its mingled mustard-seed, wild pease, and other round grains, is discharged through a tube upon the apex of a varnished wooden cone, the slopes of which are inclined to the perpendicular at an angle of about 55°. The elongated wheat-grains slide to the bottom within a certain time, being retarded by friction. The round grains, however, rolling down the side of the cone, acquire very much greater velocity, and leap across a narrow opening at the base of the cone; while the wheat-grains, moving much more slowly, fall into the opening, and are received into a separate receptacle.

The following figure (14) exhibits the working of the apparatus. The spout a is adjustable. The round grains, striking the slender ledge at the base of the cone, bound

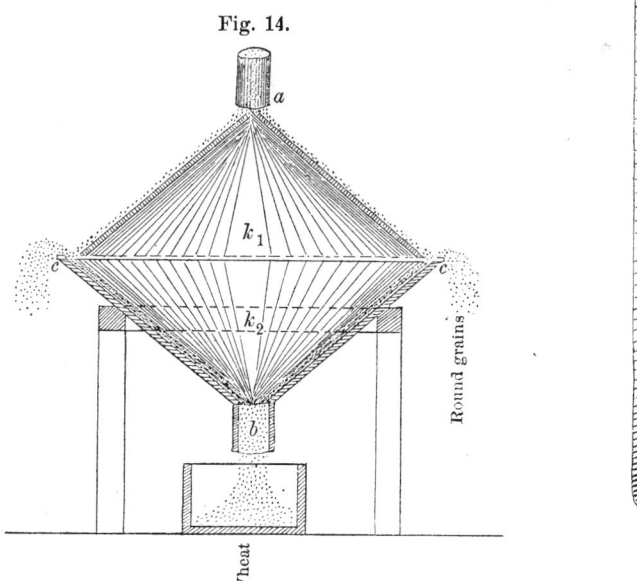

Fig. 15.

Fig. 14.

or leap across the openings c c, while the long grains of wheat, moving at a slower rate, fall through and descend the incline to b.

57. Still another device in use in the steam-mills of best repute in Austria may be mentioned. An endless apron, stretched upon two equally-inclined cylinders, receives the grain in a thin stream. The inclination is such that, as the apron moves along, the spherical grains

roll off from the lower edge of the apron, while the wheat-grains, incapable of rolling, are discharged from the apron at the curve of the cylinder.

The accompanying diagram (Fig. 15) will illustrate the construction and action of this device.

58. Another device is shown in the following diagrams, (Figs. 16, 17;) it is known as Vachon's separator. It consists of a cylinder, partly of perforated plate or wire-cloth screen and partly of peculiarly roughened surface not perforated, within which is a trough. The first part of

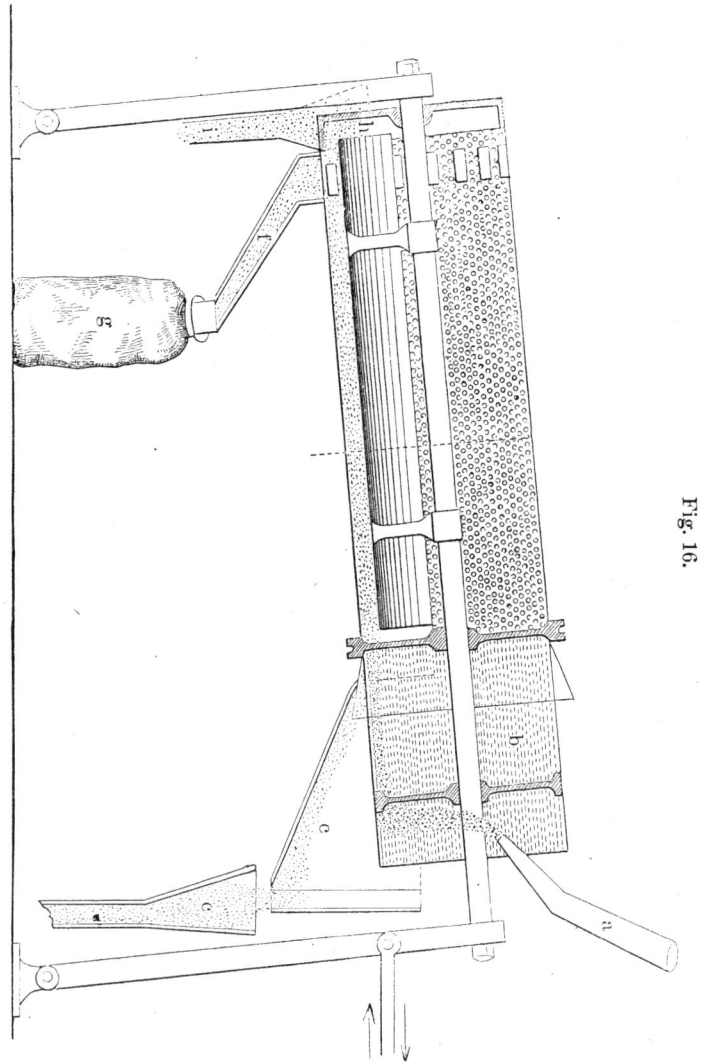

the cylinder consists of a perforated plate of such construction that only seeds smaller than the sound wheat-kernels can pass through. The remainder of the cylinder is not perforated, but is covered with a pitted surface as shown in Fig. 17. The cylinder sits loose on the axle, and is kept in slow revolution. Within the cylinder is a trough made fast to the axle, concentric with the outer cylinder, shown in Fig. 16. The cylinder has beside its slow rotation a shaking motion, and is inclined at an angle of about 10°. By means of this motion, the wheat comes at length to the end of the cylinder. It does not rise high enough on the side of the cylinder to fall into the trough, being shaken out, while the round pease and other seeds like them are carried higher, and reach the

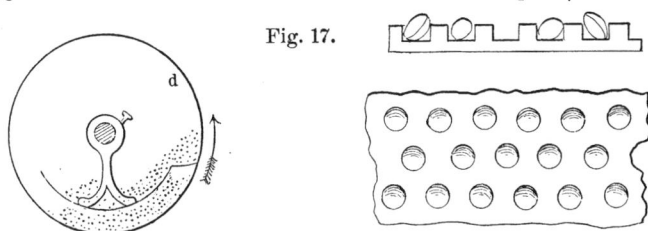

Fig. 17.

trough as they fall, and are at last discharged at $h\ i$. The wheat-grains reach the bag g; the finer particles have already been left in c. It is easy to see that while this machine may work well, as it is said to do, its yield must be small.

By these and kindred devices, and by graduated currents of air separating the shrunken or blasted kernels, the sound wheat-grain is effectually purified from all foreign substances.

59. The numerous devices on exhibition at Vienna for the purification of the grain as harvested, preparatory to the first step in milling, may all be regarded as more or less complex mechanical contrivances for the application of one or more of the principles that have been explained above.

Wheat will not "pass muster" at the Corn Exchange in Vienna when it has a musty smell, is warm, has suffered from weevil or has been worm-eaten, is blasted or is not sufficiently cleaned, or which contains more than from 3 to 5 per cent. of foreign seeds, which is to be determined by careful counting of the grains of a quarter of a pound.

60. REMOVING SMUT AND DIRT.—Washing the grain has been resorted to in the absence of facilities for removing the smut and dirt by mechanical appliances. It is true that the wheat is made by this process to look much brighter, and when the surface only is dried the grain is necessarily heavier from the absorption of water. But the absorption of water, if the wheat or the flour produced from it is to be kept any considerable length of time, is injurious from its facilitating the growth of mold and the introduction of those chemical changes which result in "heating," the disintegration of the gluten, and the general deterioration of the flour.

For drying wheat that has been washed, the apparatus of Joseph Geeman, of New York, already mentioned, which consists of a series of troughs supported in a column of heated air, with an automatic arrangement for filling and emptying, seems well suited.

61. THE UNBRANNING OF WHEAT AND THE REMOVAL OF THE BEARD.—By the mere rubbing of wheat-grains between brushes, it is not practicable to effect the complete removal of dirt and smut. Allusion has already been made to a process by which the dirt and smut together with the beard and the two outer coats of bran may be removed, with the exception of the portion contained in the bottom of the longitudinal groove on one side of the berry. This process, which may be illustrated on a small scale by rubbing a handful of moistened grains in the folds of a coarse towel, has been successfully carried out upon a large scale by a device invented by Samuel Bentz, of the United States.

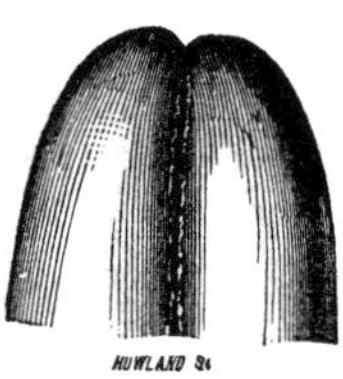

The appearance of a berry from which the outer true bran has been removed down to the gluten-coat, except the portion within the groove, by the process of Mr. Bentz, is shown in the above figure, (18.)

Fig. 18.

The accompanying diagram (Fig. 19) will show the appearance of a transverse section of wheat at the instant of unbranning, with portions of the vegetable hairs and a part of the cigar-coat wholly detached.

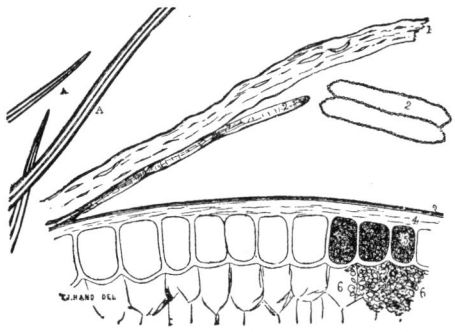

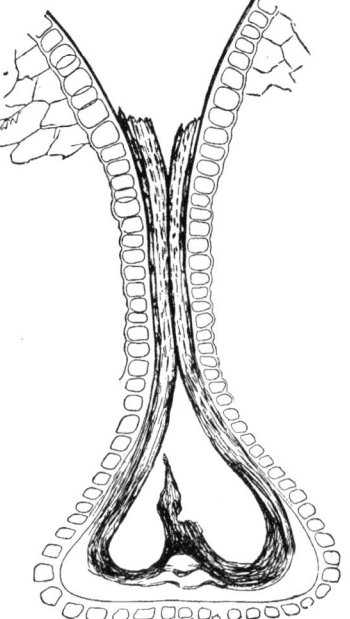

Fig. 19.—Portion of transverse section of unbranned wheat, 150 diameters.

1, 2, true bran, not yet detached at one extremity, 150 diameters.

2, detached cells of inner true bran, "cigar-coat," presenting their sides, 150 diameters.

A, A, portions of hairs from the *brush*, 100 diameters.

The annexed diagram, (Fig. 20,) like the former, from the pencil of Mr. Hand, shows the impossibility of perfectly unbranning the berry. The portion of the bran within the groove is mechanically sheltered from any effort of friction.

Fig. 20.—Transverse section of the crease of a kernel of unbranned wheat, 60 diameters. Gluten-cells in outline only.

62. SMUT-MACHINES.—Numerous devices of so-called smut-machines have been invented, in which the outer coat is more or less removed, and with it the brush, or beard. These rest in the main upon the principle of passing the wheat between sharply roughened or pointed iron sur-

PURIFYING WHEAT. 29

faces, as teeth or wire brush, or beaters upon the surface of a cylinder, or frustum of a cone, revolving at a high speed within a metallic case perforated with holes or slits, serving the double purpose of permitting the dust to escape and presenting a rough surface.

In all this department of cleaning the grain, there was a great variety of devices on exhibition at Vienna, the detailed description of which does not properly belong to this report.

The clipping of the brush and the germ at the opposite end is also effected by passing the grain between millstones, separated from each other by a distance a little less than the length of the grain and beard together. It is obvious that, in its passage between such stones, the grains will be abraded only when in position vertical to the surface of the stones.

The wheat grading and purifying machine of Howes, Babcock & Co., Silver Creek, N. Y., received the distinction of the medal of progress It is presented in section in the accompanying drawing, (Fig. 21.)

Fig. 21.

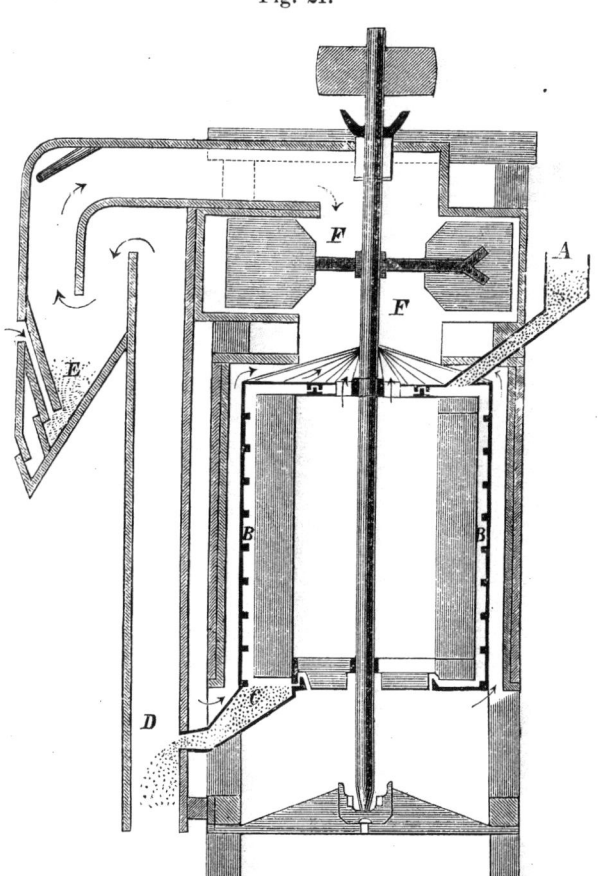

Howes, Babcock & Co.'s machine for removing smut, pointing, and cleaning grain.

The wheat enters at A, passes through the cylinder B B, comes through C to D, where it encounters the current of air produced by the exhaust-fan, which conducts the light kernels to E, the bran to F, and the fan-chamber which leads to the dust and bran chamber. The air moves in the direction indicated by the arrows. The particles of dust, hairs, smut, &c., that pass through the walls of the cylinder B B, are carried by the exhaust to F. The excellence of the work of this machine, is indorsed by Professor Kick in his official report to the Austrian government.

63. SCOURER.—Following the smut-machine, there has been introduced in some mills a *scourer*, consisting of a stiff brush, against which and below, a grooved burr-stone is made to revolve, between which the wheat passes. It serves to remove still adhering hairs and loosened portions of the outer bran, and presents, after passing through a blower, a berry of remarkable smoothness and look of purity. By this process, some varieties of wheat lose, beside the hair, portions of the outer layer of true bran, traces of the cigar-coat, and scales from the surface of the embryo.

To effect the same end in other mills, the wheat is passed between a grooved steel cylinder and a segment of a stone shell, in which the abrasion of the surface of the wheat and the partial removal of the outer bran-coat are produced. Others present a cylindrical grater operating against a surface of stone.

64. The importance of the proper conduct of the process of milling will be apparent from a simple statement found in the records of the Pesth milling.

Hungarian flour has been sent from Pesth to Trieste, and thence by sea to San Francisco and back to Trieste and Pesth, crossing the equator four times, and yet on its return found to be just as fresh, sweet, and free from anything like sour or musty smell as when it was first received from the bolt at Pesth.

To arrive at a just conception of how such flour was produced will justify the most detailed discussion of the subject.

CHAPTER II.

THE ART OF MILLING.

65. In its earliest history, the pulverization of wheat was effected by successive blows and rubbing, as in a mortar. This process involved the two effects upon the grain of varying pressure and impact. If a grain of hard wheat be subjected to pressure, as in a vise, so that its diameter shall be lessened by a certain definite amount, the interior may be partially pulverized without rupturing the surface. If the pressure reducing its diameter by the same amount be of the nature of impact or of a blow, the interior will be cracked but not pulverized, with the probable rupture of the surface. If the pressure of the vise be continued until the grain is flattened, the product will be large scales and powder. If the grain be subjected to repeated blows, sharp enough to crack but not severe enough or prolonged enough to crush, the product will be a series of fragments of various sizes, some of them having bran-scales attached.

66. Down to the beginning of this century, the construction of flouring-mills was exceedingly simple. There were a single pair of millstones and a single bolt, of which the motive power might be water or wind, horses or cattle. Everything else must be accomplished by manual labor, and the conveniences consisted of some shovels, barrels or tubs, and sieves. The wheat was usually ground in a wet condition, as moisture increased the toughness of the bran and prevented it from being reduced to fineness, and so promoted the whiteness of the flour. In the early part of this century, the first decided improvements, which ultimately resulted in the process of high milling, were made in the neighborhood of Vienna. The history of it, as given by Roman Uhl, is condensed in the following paragraphs.

67. ORIGIN OF HIGH MILLING.—The wheat was broken or cracked as finely as possible, and then the coarser parts were separated by agitating in tubs or boxes having sieves across the bottom. The bran, working to the surface because of its lightness, was from time to time separated by means of a little shovel, leaving at the bottom coarser fragments consisting of gluten, with more or less of the adhering outer coats of the bran on the one side and on the other of the interior of the berry. This material was assorted by means of sieves operated by hand, and constituted, according to Roman Uhl, the article of commerce known as Vienna grits, (Vienna *Gries.*)*

---

*Our synonyms are not perfectly suited to the case. Grits, farina, semolina, and pollard are used to distinguish the article produced. *Schrot* may be described by the roundabout phrase of broken or bruised kernels. *Unpurified grits* corresponds pretty

They were on sale in 1810 in Berlin under the same name, and were sent from the neighborhood of Wiener Neustadt (Vienna New City) to Trieste and Venice. The demand for these grits suggested the idea of coarser grinding, that is, grinding with the stones farther apart, and thus was the first step taken in the art of *grits-milling* or *high milling*.

Acts of the Austrian government in 1809 and 1810 giving freedom to the sale of flour and the erection of mills stimulated the development of milling in the neighborhood of Vienna to an unanticipated extent.

68. The recognized pioneer in invention in this direction was Ignaz Paur, born July 22, 1778, in Tattendorf, Lower Austria, died September 6, 1842, in Lichtenwörth, near Wiener Neustadt. He was first a miller in Vöslau, afterward in Schönau, and came in 1810 to Leobersdorf.

Paur made the experiment of grinding again the separated grits, and obtained a flour called from that time forward "*Auszug*," or extract flour; and such was the demand for this flour that the utmost effort to produce by hand-sifting the needed grits was inadequate to meet it.

After various experiments, he constructed, in association with a cabinet-maker by the name of Winter, the first so-called cleaning or purifying machine, attached to the bolt, and at the same time the double grits-cleaner.

69. The principle of separating the grits from the bran by means of a current of air introduced through an opening into the machine is maintained to this day, and varies but little from the device invented by Paur.

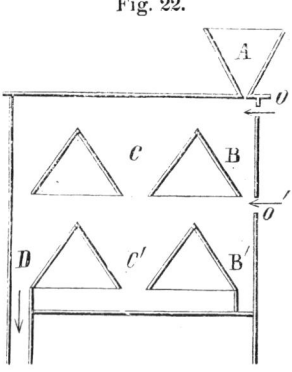

Fig. 22.

Groats or grits purifier of Ignaz Pauer.

A is the hopper, from which the broken wheat-grains fall into the purifier. O is an opening, through which a current of air is driven upon the falling fragments; the heavier fall through the division B, the next heavier fall at C, and the lighter are blown over to D. What falls through B encounters another current of air from O', which carries the lighter to C', and the heavier portion of C falls into C', while the lighter of C' and the still lighter of B' are carried over to D. Thus the fragments are resolved into three grades according to their susceptibility to be borne by the current of air.

The method of grits-milling or high milling was carried from Vienna to Hungary, Bohemia, Saxony, and elsewhere.

70. DIFFERENCE BETWEEN HIGH AND LOW MILLING.—The difference between high and low milling may be comprehensively stated to be this,

---

well with the word *middlings*. *Gries* is applied in German to the purified grits, and also to the mixture of purified grits and the bits of bran from which it has been separated in the process of purification. The terminology is at the best incomplete. I have tried to do the best I could by employing "groats" for *Schrot*, "middlings" for *Ueberschlag* or unpurified *Gries*, and "grits" for purified *Gries*.

that in high milling the wheat is reduced by a succession of crackings, or of slight and partial crushings, alternating with sifting and sorting the product, while in low milling the reduction is effected in a single crushing.

In the former, the grinding surfaces are at first remote, and are made to gradually approximate as the products become smaller. In the latter, the distance asunder of the grinding surfaces is fixed at the outset. The former may be so far separated as to merely clip the ends of the grains; they may be so near that a sheet of thick writing-paper would fill the whole space between them, and they may be separated from each other by distances anywhere between these extremes, and the products will vary accordingly.

In the high milling, the velocity of the running stone is low, while the reverse is generally true in low milling. Some varieties of wheat are better suited to the process of high milling, as the hard Hungarian wheat; others, as the softer winter or spring wheat, for example, are better suited to the process of low milling, which prevails generally in North Germany and the United States, and is believed to be more profitable to the miller, taking all the influencing circumstances into consideration, the demand for the choicer flour more especially, than high milling would be.

71. The jury on the products of milling at the Vienna Exposition took the ground that had been previously assumed at the Paris and other Expositions: that the products of high, half-high, and low milling should be judged, each class by itself, inasmuch as, already remarked, some kinds of wheat are better suited to one kind of milling and others to another.

72. HIGH MILLING, as explained by Kick in his comprehensive work, Leipsic, 1871, on "*Mehlfabrikation*," is substantially summarized as follows:

"The reduction of the wheat by the process of high milling is step by step, and the separation of the products is not alone according to the magnitude of the particles, but also according to their specific gravity.

"If one rubs grains of wheat gently between millstones, which at first are one-twelfth of an inch apart, then one-quarter less, and then one-half less, and so on, there is obtained successively a finer and finer product. By the first operation, which we will call clipping, or pointing, a part of the shell or outside coat, the brush, and more or less of the germ, will be removed, and there will be produced grains, from which already many little particles which should not appear in the flour have been separated. The outer bran and hulled kernels coming together from between the stones may be separated from each other by passing them through a cylindrical sieve. The hulled grains, by passing them next through the stones brought nearer together, yield a cracked wheat, a product consisting of various finer particles, which may be graded by sifting. The products obtained are called groats, (bruised or cracked fragments with bran attached,) grits, (smaller fragments,) and finer particles, flour. The flour obtained consists for the most part of cells and particles from the outer portion of the grain, fragments of the bran, and of the gluten-coat, which make the flour dark. It is called *pollen.*"

The grit" will consist also of a mixture of fragments of outer and inner parts, and bits of bran of the same size, which go through the sieve with the grits. A product corresponding with this somewhat, used to be called "*connell,*" and is now known as "*middlings.*"

73. The groats freed from the finer particles will be again ground, and this produces a second groats, grits, and flour; the second groats yield also groats, grits, and flour. Particles which are smaller than groats and larger than grits are called "solutions;" such as are between flour and grits are called " dust;" and these must obviously be produced by cracking. By each succeeding cracking, the flour and grits produced will consist more of particles from the *interior* of the kernel of wheat, and as the interior cells, that is, the starch-cells, yield a whiter product, so the flour and grits will become more and more fair and white; and this, until the groats after the fourth grinding will possess the form of disks, having only a thin layer of starch-cells. In flour, this phenomenon is very striking. The flour from the third groats is much fairer than that from the second or from the first groats; this is less striking in the grits, in that it is still largely mingled with particles of bran. The bran-particles are much lighter than the grits, and this property is taken advantage of to purify the grits by means of a current of air directed upon a thin sheet of falling grits. This work is accomplished by the grits-purifying machine, in which the air operates either by blast or suction.

74. In the gradual grinding and purification of the grits lies the essence of the high or grits milling. This can be effected by various modifications. The wheat may be three, four, or five times cracked or bruised ; the grits, which have been separated according to their size, may be more or less purified; and finally the purified grits may be either rapidly or slowly ground to flour.

75. In the unpurified grits, which correspond more nearly with American *middlings*, there is not only bran, which falls with it through the sieve, but there is a part of the grits, namely, the coarser, consisting of such granules as contain broken fragments of the outer part of the grain, and as such have firmly attached portions of the hull.

These particles of the hull cannot be separated by the middlings-purifying machine; and, if this is to be done, such grits must be reduced to smaller particles by passing them through properly-adjusted stones.

From the product of milling thus obtained, the flour will be bolted, and the grits subjected to a further purification.

When the last traces of bran have been separated from the grits and the still finer dust, one obtains, by grinding the pure grits and dust, the fairest, whitest flour, a product which it is impossible to obtain in any other way. Of this product, there are several grades. These flours bear the name of "extract flours," (selected or *extra* flours; and as they are obtained from the purified grits and dust of the best quality, they are also called "extract grits" and "extract dust;" and since they come from the inner parts of the grain, they bear also the name of "core-grits."

76. The grits-milling seeks to attain slowly to the pure core-grits in that at the first the outer layers are partially separated by pointing or clipping; then the clipped grains are gradually more and more reduced by bruising or cracking. In this way is obtained, as the finest product, the flour; as less fine the dust; after this the grits, solution, and groats are obtained. In all these, in relation to the size of the parts of the different products, all the elements out of which the kernel of grain is constructed are again found; all these products contain particles of the hull-bran.

The fine particles of bran in the flour which give it a dark or grayish-yellow white color cannot be separated by any means. But the case is otherwise with the grits and dust which have been purified with the grits-purifier. The larger particles remaining in the last cracking process are disk-shaped, flat, and have no longer the name of groats, but are called scales, or white stripes. They are, or should be, mainly the honey-combed coat from which the sacs of gluten and phosphates have been more or less emptied out.

The starch-cells still clinging to them will be ground off in further operation, by which finally are obtained so-called black flour and coarse bran.

The last results of milling are several kinds of flour and of bran, with which is often a part of grits, particularly finely purified, and called farina.

77. LOW MILLING.—To this process of milling stands opposed the so-called process of low milling, in which the method of production is much simpler, but the flour obtained lacks the whiteness and excellence attained by the Vienna process, or grits-milling.

In low milling, the pointed or clipped grain is passed through stones at the nearest adjustment, by which it is at once and most perfectly ground to the finest flour. It is practicable, however, by careful management of the working between the stones, to obtain a large part of bran and gluten-coats without disintegration, and to separate them from the flour by sifting, and this the more perfectly as by this process of milling finer sieves are employed. Still, it is not possible, at least it has not yet been shown, that this separation of the bran can be carried out so perfectly as to yield an "extract flour" of such fairness as is ordinarily obtained by the process of high milling.

78. In the reduction of the wheat by grinding, the end products are always flour and bran, by whatever process the milling is carried on.

The bran contains the fragments of the outer and inner bran and the gluten-coat in more finely divided form and with the least possible quantity of adhering starch-cells; such bran is called thoroughly-milled bran, and when obtained from the grits-purifying machine is called floc-bran.

79. The flour consists of starch-grains, fragments of starch-cells, with more or less splinters of the outer coats, or shell, together with the nitrogenous cells of bodies imbedded in the body of the starch.

This result obviously, with numerous differences, according to quantity and excellence, is obtained both by the high and low milling, and whether the mechanical reduction is effected by *stamping*, by *squashing*, or by *friction*. As, however, the outer layers are more coherent and tenacious than the farinaceous interior, held together in thin-walled cells, the reduction of the starch-tissues will be far advanced, while the outer portions are still in large scales. The flour produced, forming a soft medium, protects the outer parts against extreme friction, and it is for this reason impossible, by any mechanical means, to reduce the outer parts as a whole to as fine a condition as the interior mealy part. There will always be found, in the product of the mill, large scales, which, as bran, may be separated by sieves from the flour.

80. The rougher and sharper the rubbing surfaces which reduce the grain are, the more rapid and extreme is the division, as in low milling; and for this reason more of the very fine splinters, or fragments, of the outer coats are found in the product, cannot be separated by the sieve, darken the color of the flour, and make the food prepared from it less palatable.

If, on the contrary, the means for reduction are not rough, and act more by bruising, as is the case with the cylinder-mills, than by tearing, or if the common means of dividing—the millstones—are worked step by step in reduction, as takes place in the Austrian, or high-milling process, then there will be a far better and more perfect separation of the coatings possible, and the flour so produced will be finer and whiter.

81. It is obvious from what has been said that the mechanical devices for the production of flour which must be employed in every mill, group themselves in *means for division* and *means for grading*.

To these must be added the machines which are designed to purify the wheat that is to be ground, such as are employed in the separation of all foreign seeds, shrunken grains, chaff, straw, sand, and smut, the hulling or clipping machines already described, the highly important grits-purifying machines, employed in the grits or high milling, and which, as employed in the low milling or half-high milling in the United States, are known as the middlings-purifiers; and finally certain other co-operating devices for the cooling and preservation of the product, and for facilitating its transportation.

82. MILLSTONES.—There were, on exhibition at Vienna, millstones in great number and variety; some of them were of single blocks or hard stones, including sandstones, basalt, and lava, porphyry and granite.

There were, besides, the burr or French stones composed of fragments of siliceous sinter of varying compactness or porosity, cemented together, which, on account of their hardness and the sharpness of their angles and their porosity yielding sharp edges, are universally preferred to all others, both in Europe and America.

83. Invention has been directed with more or less success in recent times to effect the grinding by the rotation of the lower stone only, and by the rotation in opposite directions of the lower and upper millstones; but, on account of its convenience in facilitating the sharpening of the grooves, the almost universal practice is to confine the movement to the upper stone.

84. The surface of the stone is technically made up of the eye, the bosom, and the skirt; the eye being at the center. The accompanying diagram exhibits the several parts.

Fig. 23.

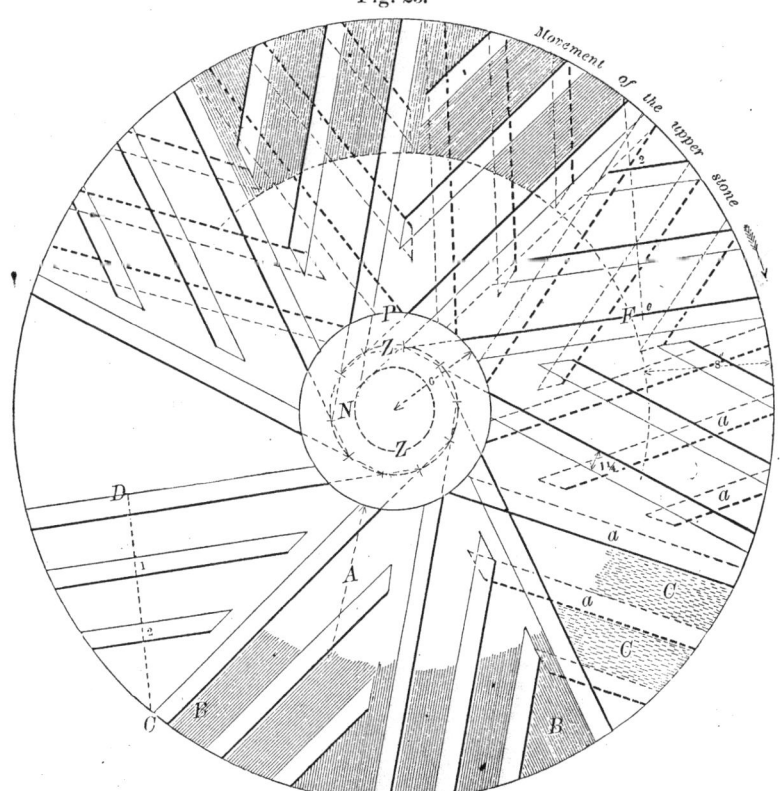

Surface of stone, with furrows in ten quarters, for high milling. The furrows in dotted outline, *a a*, indicate the upper or running stone; A, the bosom, which is slightly dished toward the eye; B B, the finely-grooved surface of the lands of the skirt of the under stone; C C, the grooved lands of the running stone.

85. The action of the grooves and lands of the upper and lower stones upon each other may be illustrated with the aid of the dia-

gram, (Fig. 23.) The dotted diagram may represent the surface of the lower stone, while the diagram of continuous lines will represent the upper or running stone. It will be seen now, as the eye follows the intersection of any two curves, that the movement of the upper stone will carry the point of intersection to the circumference of the lower stone, as the point of intersection of operating shears is carried from the hinge to the point.

The accumulated meal will be continually pushed forward and outward by the joint action of the upper stone upon the lower and the centrifugal force.

It will be noticed that the grooves, or furrows, which, with the lands, occupy the bosom and skirt of the stone, are of two kinds, long and short. The long ones are not sections of radii from the center, but are tangents from the circumference of interior circles; the short furrows are parallel to the long furrows. The chief grinding surfaces lie in the outer half or skirt; the area of the lands equals or somewhat exceeds that of the furrows. The furrows, instead of being straight, are sometimes curved, as in the following figures:

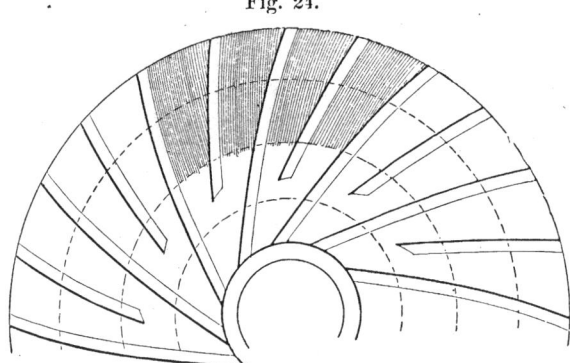

Fig. 24.

Sketch showing circular grooves of recent device.

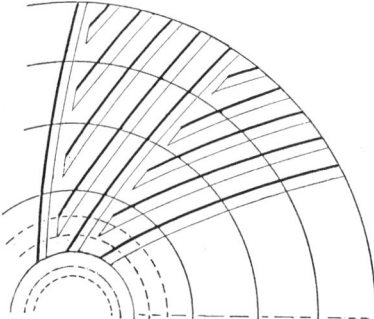

Fig. 25.

The Evans grooves; logarithmic spirals.

These curves are sometimes sectors of circles, sometimes cutting the eye of the stone, and sometimes tangent to it, and in the more recent and improved curved grooves they are sections of logarithmic spirals.

86. The object of the furrows is twofold: first, to provide rough surfaces for the disintegration of grain, tearing or cracking or rubbing; and, secondly, for providing channels for the movement of the crushed grain toward the circumference.

The finer grooves on the lands facilitate the detaching of the friable interior portion of the fragments from the tougher shell. They also serve in giving rotation to the fragments, and thus expose the projecting points to the abrasion of the revolving stone.

87. The accompanying diagram (Fig. 26,) from Kick, illustrates an approved form of the groove; the arrow gives the direction in which the upper stone moves. The depth and width of the furrows are those of the stones in the Thilenius Mill of Cape Girardeau, Missouri.

Fig. 26.

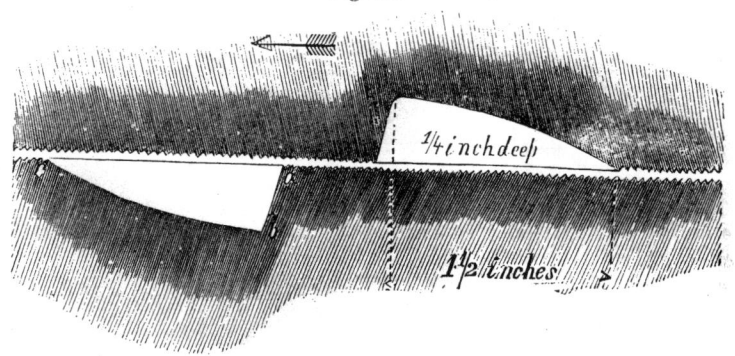

It will be seen that the pulverized grain as it accumulates in the trough *a b c*, will be pushed up along the surface *b c* to the summit of the finely-grooved land beyond, where it will be subjected to trituration till it reaches the next furrow, from which it will, as the furrow fills, be forced out on to the succeeding land.

88. The pulverized or ground grain is discharged from the skirt under the influence of the centrifugal force; the velocity of its movement increasing with the distance from the center. This velocity may be checked by nearing the stones to each other, or it may be checked by the conformation of the furrows toward the periphery.

In low milling, with a given velocity of the running stone, the centrifugal force will obviously be antagonized by friction more than in the high milling, and the heat consequent upon the friction will be greater. The temperature of the flour issuing from the stones in ordinary low milling is found to be in the total flour about 120° Fahrenheit.

It is manifest that inasmuch as some portion of the flour, the fine particles for example, are less subjected to friction, other portions, as the gluten-cells, which are larger, must be heated to a very much higher temperature than 120°. To this heat is largely due the vapor of water, which is known to be disengaged in the process of low milling. This doubtless comes from the gluten, which is known to be a hydrate, which parts with its water at a temperature considerably below the temperature of boiling water. This suggests that possibly the accepted superiority of the extract flour by the high-milling process is due to the circumstance that the gluten which it contains has been subjected to less heat and less consequent deterioration than the gluten of the flour produced in the low-milling process. To this point attention will be further directed in considering the adaptation of different grades of flour to the production of bread.

89. The following diagrams (Fig. 27) exhibit various forms of furrows that have been produced in the development of the art of milling.

Fig. 27.

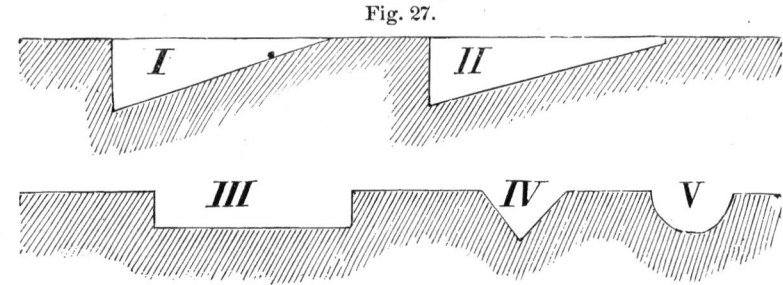

90. The outline of the furrows in their length and section, the comparative breadth of the furrows and lands, the depth of the skirt, and the fine grooving of the lands, the dishing of the bosom, the distance apart of the stones, and the velocity of the runner—all have relations, independent and combined, to the qualities of the grain to be ground; on the most careful attention to which and to the condition of the moisture or dryness of the air depends the successful prosecution of the art of milling. In no other country has such an amount of scientific research been given to this subject as in Hungary, and there very extraordinary results have been obtained.

91. In different mills, these elements are variously combined, some holding tenaciously to the logarithmic spiral, others insisting upon the superiority of the straight furrow, some giving only the faintest dishing to the bosom or none at all, and others limiting the grinding surface to less than the outer half of the milling surface.

In the Istvan steam-mills at Debreczin, under the direction of Prof. E. Pekár, with the stones 54 inches in diameter, and skirt or grinding surface but 9 inches in width, measuring from the periphery along the radius, the very highest order of results has been obtained.

92. In a well-appointed flouring-mill in Brooklyn, N. Y., where low milling is practiced, in which high grades of flour are produced, the furrows have a depth of from three-sixteenths to a quarter of an inch, and are 1½ inches wide; the stones are 4 feet 4 inches in diameter. The long lands are 1¾ inches wide at the circumference, and the short lands 2¾.* The curves of the principal furrows are logarithmic spirals.

93. The following diagram (Fig. 28) is a copy of the face of the stone of the Thilenius Mill at Cape Girardeau, Missouri, which produced the flour exhibited at the Vienna Exposition. It has been furnished, together with details of the process, in reply to questions addressed to Mr. Thilenius by me.

The dimensions are as follows: The furrows are 1½ inches wide and

---

* The areas of furrows and of lands are about equal; the lands being perhaps a little larger. The top stone corresponds with the lower exactly in its dressing

SURFACE OF STONE OF THILENIUS MILL.

¼ of an inch deep. The small lands are 2¾ inches, the others 2 inches wide. The fine grooving of the lands extends from 10 to 12 inches from the periphery toward the center, and has from 30 to 35 creases or fine grooves to an inch. The bush is 10 inches square and the spindle 4

Fig. 28.

Stone 4 feet in diameter; cutting surface, 13 quarters; fine grooving (skirt) extends from 10 to 12 inches from the periphery and has from 30 to 35 cracks to 1 inch; bush 10 inches square; spindle 4 inches.

inches in diameter. The bed-stone and runner are dished $\frac{1}{48}$ of an inch toward the center. The stones are 4 feet in diameter and make 160 revolutions per minute. The flour as it issues has a temperature of from 110° to 126° Fahrenheit.

94. The next figure (29) exhibits a grain of wheat about to be cracked and crushed by the movement of the upper stone.

The motion from left to right will carry the fragments up the inclined plane to the land, where they will be reduced to a size determined by the distance apart of the stones.

Fig. 29.

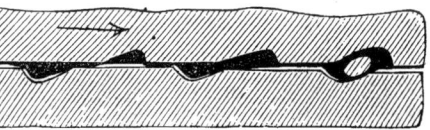

95. VENTILATION.—The passage of the wheat from the eye to the grinding-surfaces has been facilitated by a blast of air accompanying the falling grain from the hopper, which serves also to cool the product in the process of grinding. It tends, however, to accumulate the pulverized grain in the path of the blast, and so, by increasing the friction, to neutralize the cooling effect. The quantity of flour produced in a given time is, nevertheless, largely increased. An experiment is recorded in which, without ventilation, seven pairs of millstones ground hourly fourteen hundred and forty-eight pounds of wheat, while with ventilation two thousand and seventy-eight pounds were ground with four pairs of stones in the same time, a ratio in favor of ventilators as nearly 5 : 2. The coal consumed by these two processes showed a saving with ventilation of 23 per cent. The trustworthiness of these results is questioned by Professor Kick. The ventilation may be effected either by a blast from compressed air; by suction—drawing the air from the eye to the circumference; by a combination of blast and suction; or by the introduction of air between the grinding-surfaces through openings in the running stone. This expedient is not resorted to—as it is not needed—in the Hungarian milling.

96. THE COOLING OF THE FLOUR.—The temperature of the pulverized product as it issues from between the stones has already been alluded to as a consequent of the friction attendant upon the process of grinding. The ventilation, mingling a current of air with the pulverized grain, tends to restore the normal temperature. This principle is applied on a larger scale after the grinding, where mechanical appliances are introduced to stir the meal, and continually bring fresh surfaces in contact with the air. The familiar hopper-boy, which is a sort of great rake, so operated as to stir up a layer of meal of moderate depth, has been adopted from America into Germany.

97. As the friction is greater and the temperature higher in the low-milling than in the high-milling process, the necessity of cooling the product of the former is greater. Indeed, such cooling has been deemed indispensable to the preservation of the flour. In the high-milling process, where the quantity of flour produced to a single pair of stones is relatively small, no special arrangement for cooling is necessary, since the alternate grinding and bolting, as the successive steps of the process advance, prevent the temperature of the product from rising above the margin of safety.

98. THE CYLINDER-MILLING.—This is more especially true of the cylinder-milling, where the successive steps in the reduction of the wheat are very numerous and alternate regularly with the cooling process. The cylinder or roller mill, or *Walzenmühle*, of the Hungarians consists in its simplest elements of two small parallel, horizontally-disposed steel cylinders, placed near to each other, arranged for adjustment, and revolving from above toward each other. The cylinders in the great Pesth *Walzenmühle*, the flour from which won the highest distinction at Vienna,

HUNGARIAN WALZ-MÜHLE.

were not more than five inches in diameter; the surfaces of some of them were traversed by numerous sharp furrows, or, which is the same thing, numerous sharp ridges parallel to the axis; others were smooth.

99. The accompanying diagram (Fig. 30) exhibits three pairs of roll-

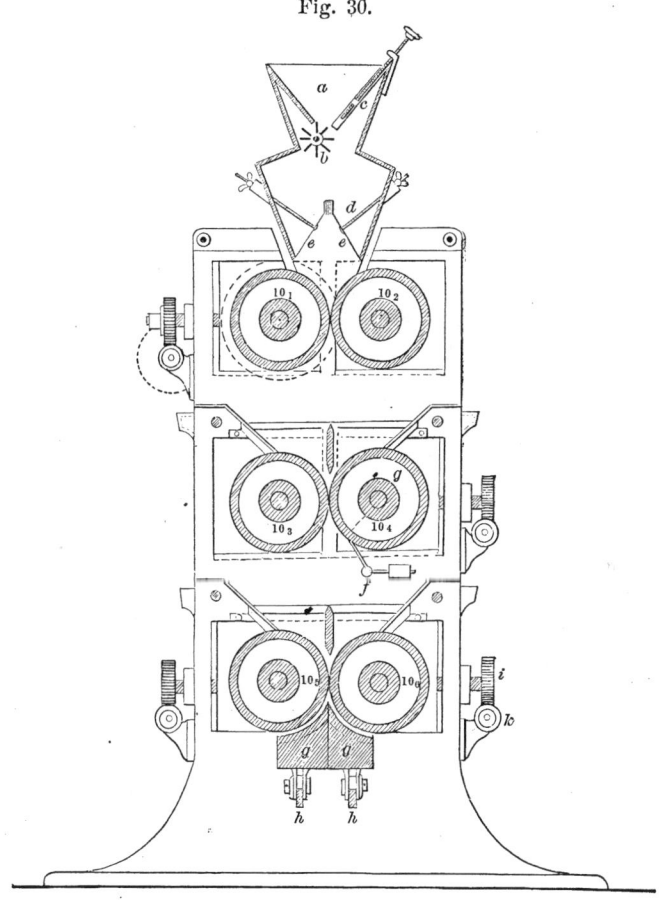

Fig. 30.

ers, one above another, in a set, showing how the grain, in passing from one pair of cylinders to the next, passes through an intervening body of air, and how the slight heat developed by the pressure between one pair of cylinders may be overcome by the cooling effect of the air through which it passes on its way to the next pair of cylinders.

The smooth cylinders, revolving with uniform speed, if near enough together would crush the grain to flatness; if revolving with unequal velocity, the tendency would be to squash the grain; with grooved cylinders, the tendency is to indent and crack the grain where the velocity of the two cylinders is the same. Where the fluted or furrowed rollers revolve with unequal velocities, the action is frictional. The action depends as well upon their distance from each other as upon the character of their surface.

100. If smooth cylinders are so far apart that the pressure is but slight, the berry will split open along the groove throughout its length, the two halves frequently clinging together, somewhat suggesting an open book; if the cylinders are nearer together, soft wheat will be flattened, hard wheat will be cracked into fragments, and the grits will be freer from bran than when obtained by grinding between stones. The following diagram (Fig. 31) presents a profile of the grooved surface of a roller of large diameter:

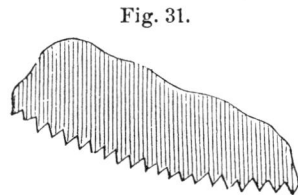

Fig. 31.

101. The essential advantage of the *Walz* or cylinder milling is that the product is *not heated*; it is a process of cold milling. It is also to be remarked that there is no dust-flour produced.

In the great Pesth *Walzenmühle*, under the direction of Dosswald of the international jury, the wheat, before attaining its last disintegration, passed through from eighteen to twenty-four pairs of cylinders. The product of grits, flour of various grades, and bran was obtained from the Hungarian commissioner at the Exposition, and analyses have been made, which will appear in their proper place farther on.

102. In Wyngaert's journal "*Die Mühle*," of December, 1874, and January, 1875, an account is given of an improved *Walzenmühle*, the work of an Italian inventor, Wegmann, in which the cylinders are of porcelain and the space between the cylinders controlled by springs, (formerly by levers and weights as shown in the diagrams,) which, in the judgment of Wyngaert, promises to be of great value.

Wyngaert says there is practically no heating of the product, and that the gluten retains its normal qualities; that the bran is subjected to no tearing process, but is flattened out, and the interior portion pressed away so that the middlings-purifier is rendered unnecessary; that the yield of first flour is greatly increased; that the effect of the adoption of the porcelain *Walzenmühle* on the low milling will be to change it to half-high milling; and the effect of it on high milling will be to reduce the number of grades of flour, a consummation greatly to be desired.

Wyngaert sums up the advantages of Wegmann's porcelain-cylinder mill, as shown in a series of special experiments undertaken at his instance and under his direction, as follows:

1. It renders unnecessary the whole system of grits and middlings purifiers.

2. It secures a larger proportion of clear, pure flour.

3. It makes it impossible to injure the quality of the flour in milling.

103. The accompanying figures illustrate in some degree the construction of the porcelain-cylinder mill.

WEGMANN'S PORCELAIN-CYLINDER MILL.

Fig. 32 is a sectional view. Fig. 33 is a view from above. Fig. 34 is a side-view. In Fig. 32, a shows the feed-cylinder; b, the porcelain cyl-

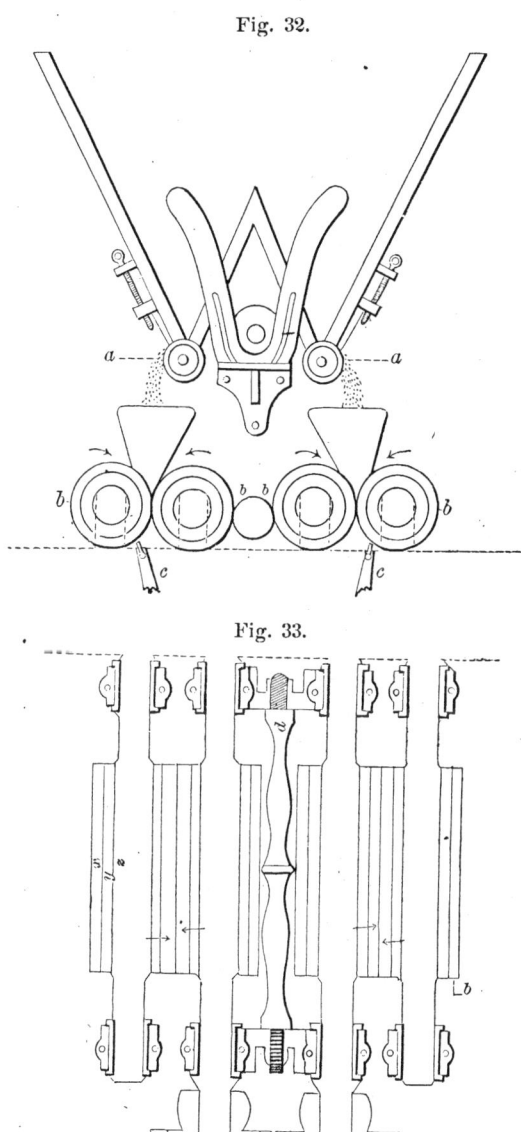

Fig. 32.

Fig. 33.

inders; c, the scraper with glass-edge. In Fig. 33, d shows the coupling-bolts of the uprights; x, the porcelain shell; y, the lead interior shell; e, the axle. In Fig. 34, b is the porcelain shell; c, the scraper, with the weight e to secure the glass edge against the porcelain surface. The figures are one-tenth the size of the actual machinery.

Fig. 34.

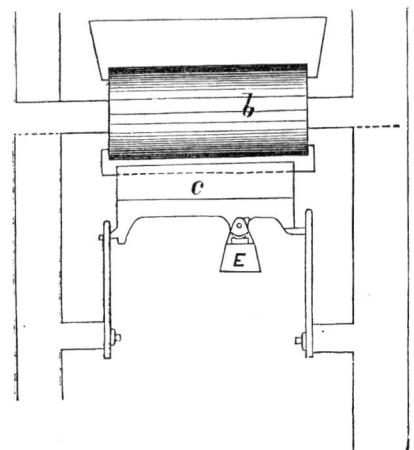

104. The *Walzenmühle*, or grits-mill, with one cylinder, from the St. Georgen Manufactory at St. Gallen, was on exhibition. It is presented in the accompanying figure, (35.)

Fig. 35.

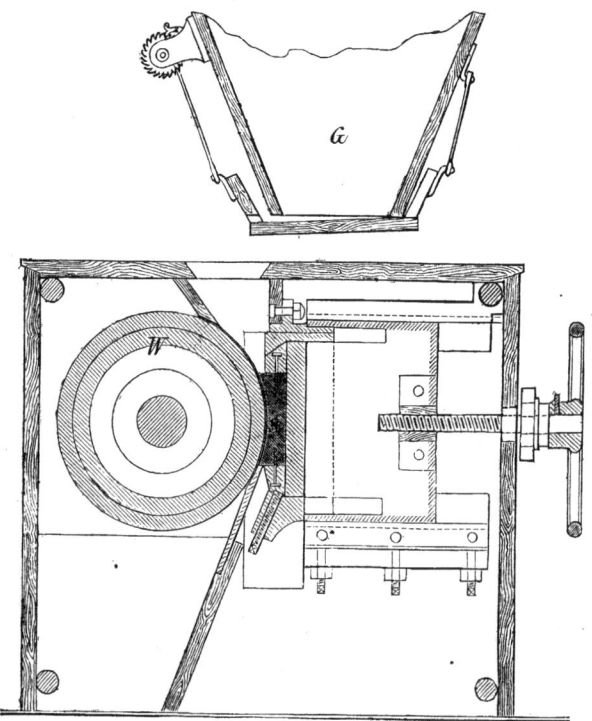

Cylinder-mill of St. Georgen, St. Gallen, Switzerland.

DISINTEGRATOR. 47

W is the cylinder, with steel shell, and S is the steel concave. It is used only for the purpose of cracking the grain and the production of grits, leaving the further milling to be pursued with runs of stones.

105. DISINTEGRATOR.—Beside the two great systems of milling— the high (I) and low, (II,) which differ from each other in the distance apart of the upper and lower stones, and the *Walz* or cylinder milling, (III,) there is (IV) a system of disintegration, in which there are neither stones nor cylinders, but in which the pulverization is effected by friction of the grain upon itself, the wheat being kept in motion by beaters revolving at high velocity in a hollow cylinder. The product in a given time with a given expenditure of power is said to be very large. It has not been widely introduced.

Fig. 36.

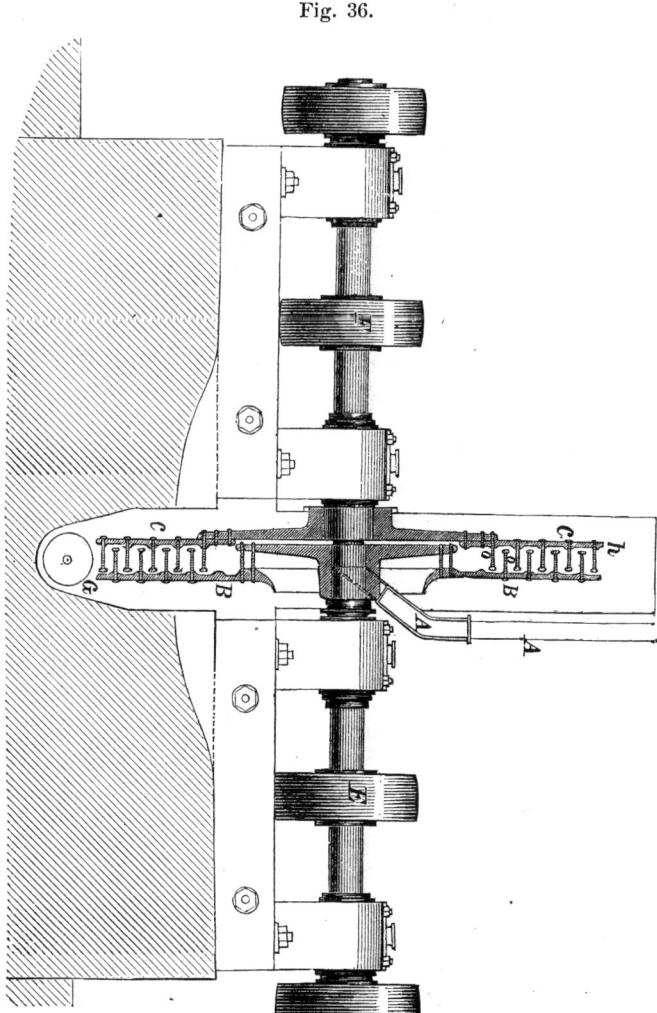

Carr's disintegrator, or centrifugal mill.

Kick's Vienna Report, after analyzing the work of Carr's centrifugal disintegrator, gives it a secondary place, as compared with the work of the high milling with runs of stone or the cylinder-mill. The diagram (Fig. 36) exhibits a section of one of the forms of this apparatus at the Exposition.

106. SUMMARY.—The extreme *low* milling is a system of *mashing* and repeated scraping and squeezing and a single bolting. It is attended with heating of the product, which injures the flour.

The *high* milling is a system of successive crackings with alternate removal of the finer particles and the bran as fast as produced. It is attended with but little heating of the product. There is some cracking in low milling and some mashing in high milling.

The *half-high* milling, as its name imports, partakes more of the cracking than low milling, and more of the scraping and squeezing than high milling.

The cylinder-milling is a system of pressing and cracking, and, where the cylinders are grooved and move with unequal velocities, of tearing. Like the high milling, it produces little heat.

107. SIFTING OR BOLTING OF THE PRODUCTS OF GRINDING.—The bolting process to which the product of the grinding is subjected immediately after cooling, has for its object in the low-milling process to get the largest possible amount of flour, and of course the smallest amount of bran.

In high milling, bolting or sifting has various objects to accomplish. As the grain is reduced by successive grindings into groats, grits, and flour, between each two steps in the grinding process there must be one or more gradings, boltings, or siftings to separate the products from each other; and, to complete the process, sieves of varying degrees of fineness are employed; the coarser sieves may be made of wire, but all the finer ones are for the most part of silk.

The sizes of the openings in the bolting-cloth vary from three hundred and twenty-four in the square inch to more than twenty thousand. The number of meshes in a square inch is indicated by certain numbers qualifying the fineness of the bolting-cloth, and these numbers should be employed to indicate the flour which passes through the meshes of the corresponding numbers of the cloth. But, unfortunately, this is not the case; the numbering of the flours is quite arbitrary.

The numbers upon the wire-cloth and the grits silk gauze indicate the number of meshes in a linear inch. The numbers of the silk bolt-cloth are entirely arbitrary.

108. BRAN-DUSTER.—The brush-sieve consists of a wire-gauze cylinder; within this fixed drum is a revolving axle making from two hundred and fifty to two hundred and seventy revolutions in a minute, and carrying with it cast-iron rings, at the circumference of which is attached a series of bars bearing brushes. The office of the brushes is

THE FLOUR-BOLT.

to rub off the flour from the bran, and drive the flour through the fine wire-gauze, while the bran is permitted to pass on.

109. The proportion of flour of the white interior of the grain adhering to ordinary miller's bran, before subjection to the bran-duster, is indicated in the accompanying cut, (Fig. 37.)

Fig. 37.

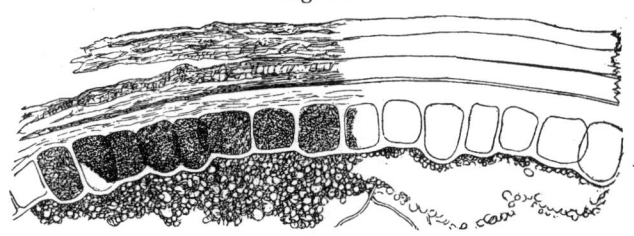

Transverse section of a scale of millers' bran, magnified to 150 diameters ; drawn under the Camera Lucida, part being left in outline only.

110. THE FLOUR-BOLT.—The construction of the flour-bolt, whether round or hexagonal, whether single or double, whether in connection with interior screws for the movement of the flour, and the disposition of the bolting-cloth of different degrees of fineness, would lie without the scope of the present report.

The problem presenting itself in the separation of the various products resulting from the processes of reduction in high milling will be apparent from a consideration of the following diagrams. They illustrate at a glance some of the important stages through which the grain passes on its way from wheat to flour and bran.

Fig. 38 exhibits the result of the first cracking of the berry or pointing. The stones were at the maximum distance apart for removing the brush. The product has been freed from the hairs or bristles, more or less of the outer bran-scales, fine flour, and whatever minute particles had been detached in running through the stones. It is purified. In Fig. 39, we have the result of the second cracking, purified.

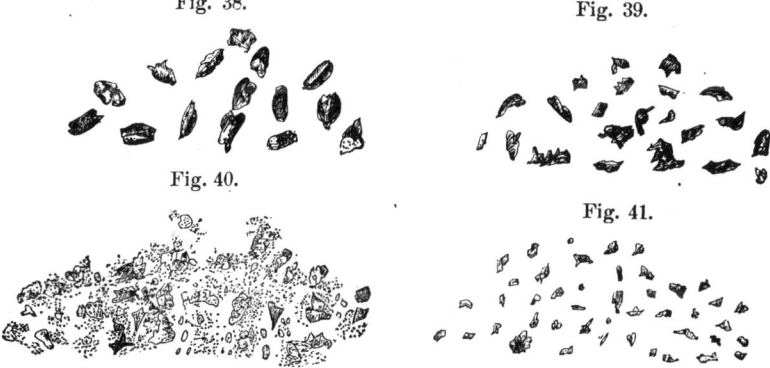

Fig. 38.   Fig. 39.

Fig. 40.   Fig. 41.

In Fig. 40, we have the product of the fourth cracking, precisely as it came from between the stones. One sees what was the condition of the grits of Fig. 43 and Fig. 45 before they were purified. In Fig. 41, we

4 V B

have the coarse solution, a mixture of groats and grits. In Fig. 42, we have the *medium solution*—of groats and grits.

In Fig. 43, we have grits No. 1, or farina, or semolina; and, in Fig. 45, we have grits much finer—No. 5.

In Fig. 44, we have the bran, which has been ground and scrubbed, and as far as possible exhausted to the gluten-coat.

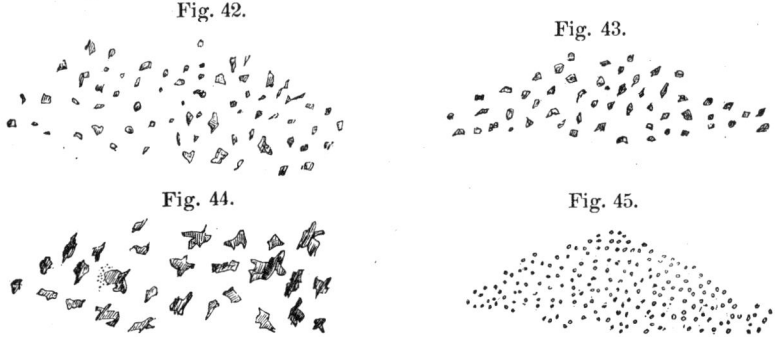

Fig. 42.   Fig. 43.   Fig. 44.   Fig. 45.

111. THE PURIFICATION OF THE GRITS.—The separation of the grits from the bran-scales of equal size is so distinctly of Austrian or Hungarian origin, and so essential to the production of the high grades of flour from which the excellent Vienna bread is produced, as to justify the attempt to present an outline of some of the principal devices by which this separation is effected. These products differ from each other in essential particulars. The bran is the shell of the wheat. The grits are fragments from the interior.

To the bran proper, there are adhering much of the gluten-coat and some of the starch of the interior. To the grits, there are sometimes still adhering portions of the gluten and occasionally of the other outer coats of the wheat.

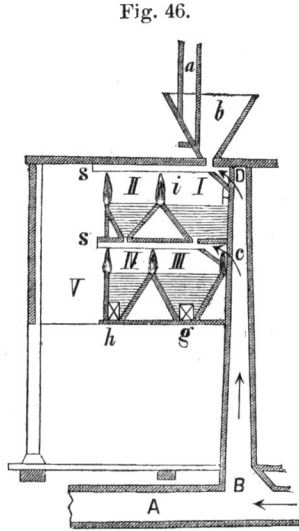

Fig. 46.

112. The bran is thin and flat, or consists of scales; the grits are irregular fragments of the grain, roundish or granular. The bran is specifically lighter than the grits, and presents, relatively to its weight, a much greater extent of surface.

Upon these differences rest the separation of the bran from the grits. The agencies employed are, first, the current of air, produced either by blast or suction; and, secondly, centrifugal force.

The current of air is directed against a thin stream of falling mixed bran and grits. All the particles are blown out of the perpendicular—the heaviest least, the lightest most. The bran, presenting the largest amount of surface with a given amount of material, is driven farthest;

the grits, presenting a less extent of surface relative to the amount of material, fall nearest to the perpendicular. Between these is an intermediate portion.

The preceding cut (Fig. 46) exhibits a machine substantially the device of Ignaz Paur, the discoverer of the process of high milling. It has been already partially described. *b* is a hopper having a long narrow slit at the bottom. *a* is a flat supply-tube, with an adjustable slide for the supply of the mixed bran and grits. Through the opening *d*, a current of air encounters the cascade of falling bran and grits. The grits fall into the division *I*, the bran is carried on to the division *V*, and the intermediate portion falls into the division *I I*. The current of air entering at *c* subjects the grits and intermediate portion from *I* and *I I* to a second purifying operation.

Bauer's exhaust grits-purifier and Escher Wys's grits-purifier are selected by Professor Kick in his report on Group IV to the Austrian government, from the vast number on exhibition. They are shown in the diagrams, (Fig. 47 and Fig. 48.) It may be questionable whether such extreme grading of products as must result in Bauer's apparatus is desirable.

Fig. 47.

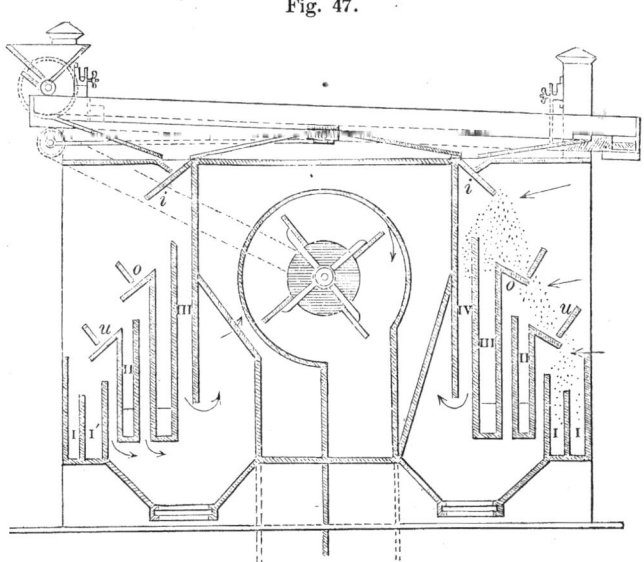

Bauer's exhaust grits purifier.

113. In the great *Walzmühle* at Pesth, there was an apparatus which the annexed diagram (Fig. 49) will illustrate: A is a hopper receiving the meal; B is a cylinder fitting the spout from the hopper and admitting of raising or lowering; *b* is a circular, smooth, metallic plate revolved by a vertical shaft attached below. The meal, as it issues from the foot of the hollow cylinder with increasing velocity, is carried to the periphery, and shot outward into a current of air produced by suction through the spout H. The rounded grits, having greatest weight in proportion to

the extent of surface, reach the space D; the bran-flakes, having least material to surface, are drawn to F; and the fine flour falls between to the receptacle H.

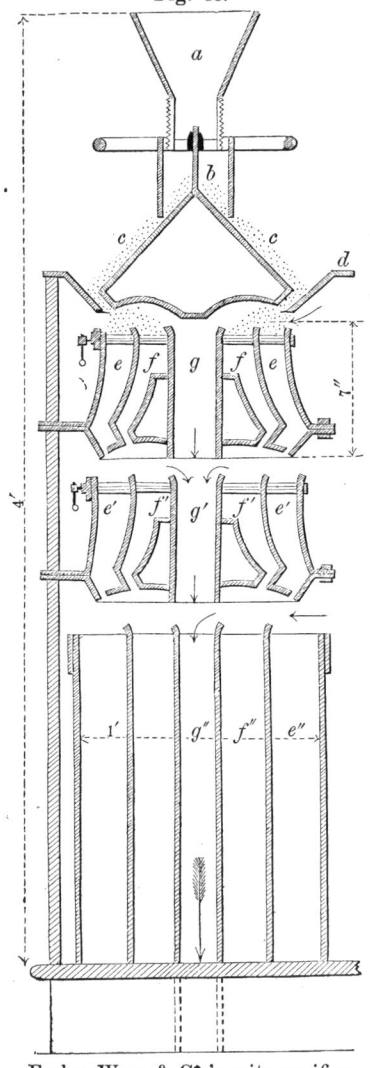

Fig. 48.

Escher Wyss & Cº.'s grits purifier.

114. Another device has been contrived for separating the minute bran-scales from the grits of equal size, by causing a broad stream of air, either by blast or suction, to pass through a slightly-inclined plane sieve of meshes sufficiently large for both the bran and grits to pass through; the force of the blast being so gentle as to permit the grits to drop, while the particles of bran are kept afloat to be discharged at the lower margin of the sieve. The sieve is sometimes disposed around a cylinder, and the action promoted by a brush acting upon the surface of the sieve in connection with the blast or suction. Of this class, several of most ingenious construction, under the name of middlings-purifiers, have been recently invented and brought into use in this country. The accompanying figure (50) illustrates one of the simpler forms.

aa, the slightly-inclined sieve, through which the air is carried upward by the exhaust-fan, by which the fine bran is

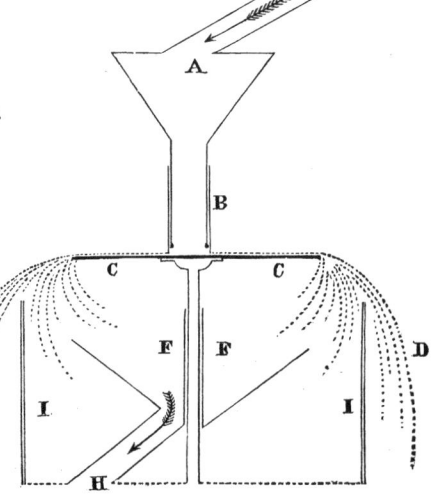

Fig. 49.

prevented from passing through, while the heavier purified middlings are dropped to the trough below.

115. THE PRODUCTS OF THE TWO PROCESSES OF LOW MILLING AND HIGH MILLING.—The relative merits of these two modes of milling have been discussed at great length and with signal ability by the Austrian and German millers. Foremost among those in asserting and expounding the just claims of the process of low milling with its recent and most improved appliances is the distinguished Joseph J. van den Wyngaert, editor of the German journal "*Die Mühle*," and member of the international jury, Group IV, Division— Flour and its Products, &c. In his numerous papers, he has set forth with great clearness and force the principle that the question of relative superiority is not to be determined upon purely scientific principles alone; but that inasmuch as milling, as a great practical art, is intimately connected with the every-day life of the whole community, it must be first of all self-sustaining; it must provide a flour for which there is sufficient demand to yield a living-profit to the miller, over and above the cost of the grain and its working, including the various tariffs, the interest upon capital, and the expense for repairs; in other words, that it will not do to produce an article, however attractive to the scientific mind, for which there is little or no remunerating demand on the part of consumers. In the second place, he holds that inasmuch as the Austro-Hungarian process of disintegration of tissues is a process of successive crackings, it is especially suited to a hard and brittle wheat, which is the principal wheat in the markets of Vienna and Pesth, and is not suited to the softer varieties of wheat, which are more abundant in North Germany, England, and the United States, and which consist of a tougher shell and a more mealy and friable interior. He cites instances in which mills erected with the appliances for high milling, because of their not being found self-sustaining, have been converted into mills with the conveniences for low milling.

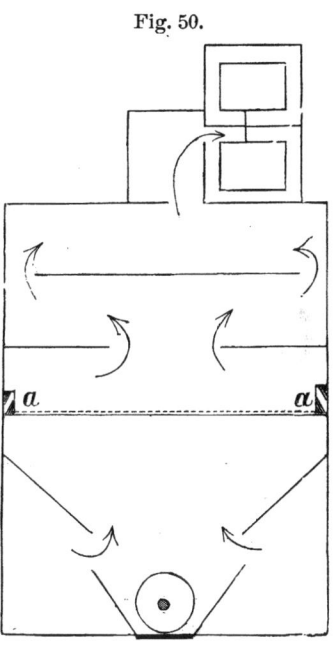

Fig. 50.

He presents ("*Stenographischer Bericht der sechsten Versammlung deutscher Müller und Mühlen-Interessenten*") a series of tables illustrating the production of various high and low milling establishments in Baden and Bavaria, with the cost of wheat ground, the amounts and kinds of products turned out, the cost of grinding and fitting for market, and the receipts from sales, in which the profits of the low milling are, according to the figures, decidedly greater. He submits also the result of a series of experiments in baking with the different kinds of flour, and reaches the conclusion from them and from the relative profits, that low milling, at least for the wheat of Northern Germany, that is, as of softer wheat distinguished from hard, is more profitable than high milling would be.

He dwells upon the fact that the hard, flinty wheat is chiefly a matter of climate, and that crops in the same district vary in their hardness on the different soils and even in the same fields in different years, and to some extent according to the character of the preceding crops.

Wyngaert gives due prominence, in seeking an explanation of the excellence of the Vienna bread, also to the beautiful white press-yeast with which the Austro-Hungarian bakers are supplied.

116. The physical impracticability of producing lumps from the friable interior of the soft wheat shows at a glance the inferior adaptation of this kind of wheat to the production of the numerous grades of grits which characterize the Austro-Hungarian milling. The toughness of the shell of the soft wheat makes it practicable to obtain a product in low milling in which the fine particles of bran are relatively few, and from which a flour of high order of whiteness may be obtained. The dry, brittle Hungarian wheat, subjected to the low-milling process, would, by reason of the brittleness of the shell, yield a product in which the small particles of bran would be numerous, and, being of the same size, would pass through the bolt with the flour, and make it impossible to produce a flour of perfect whiteness. By moistening the Hungarian wheat, however, before grinding, the toughness of the shell would be increased, its reduction to fine particles in the process of grinding would be less, and the flour would be made whiter.

117. The advocates of high milling rest upon the claims of the scientific solution of the problem: the reduction of the wheat-grain by a succession of alternate crackings and sortings, in which disintegration is effected by successive steps of such slight individual advance, and the graduations of the successive products are so fine that the heat produced is inconsiderable, and the ultimate product of flour free from specks and of absolute fairness is much larger than by the low-milling process. The significance of this peculiarity of the process cannot be easily overestimated. It leaves the integrity of the cells of gluten unimpaired. They have, therefore, their natural investment of cellular tissue to protect the sensitive nitrogenous constituents of the interior from the oxygen of the air, and from the spores of microscopic vegetation always afloat in the atmosphere. Having escaped destructive crushing, they have also escaped the heat attendant upon it, and the loss of water and chemical decomposition due to it. As the chemical changes consequent upon this exposure of the gluten bring with them products of disagreeable taste and smell, the flour produced by the high milling has escaped the deterioration consequent upon the destruction of the texture of the gluten-cells.

118. From the researches of Mégé Mouriès, already referred to, it would appear that the gluten-comb of the grain contains a nitrogenous constituent of great susceptibility to fermentation upon the application of water, in which it is soluble. This body, so long as the cells containing the gluten remain intact, is protected from the moisture of the air. The importance of maintaining these cells unbroken in the flour until it is to be converted into bread needs no illustration.

The defense of the theory of high milling, where the hardness of the grain renders it practicable, seems perfect.

119. The inferior adaptation of the process of high milling to the softer varieties of wheat has led to a compromise between the two processes, called half-high milling, already referred to, in which the advantages of the principles of high milling are recognized and the necessary profits of the miller to make his art self-sustaining are maintained.

120. After all that may be written, one is forcibly impressed with the conviction that, as in every kindred case, there will remain an unwritten art, which is only to be acquired by actual contact day by day, for long periods, with all the details of the business.

In the art of the miller, it must continue from the selection of the grain to the sale of the flour, upon which scientific treatment and commercial success depend and are made to harmonize with each other.

121. PROPORTIONS OF THE DIFFERENT GRADES OF FLOUR YIELDED BY THE HIGH AND LOW MILLING PROCESSES.—By the processes of low milling, we have the following scheme of treatment:

Table showing the course of ordinary low milling.

Cleaning.
Clean wheat.   Refuse.

Pointing.
Pointed wheat.   Poorest flour.   Coarse bran.

Grinding.
Flour No. 3, or No. 2. / No. 1. / No. 3.   Dust.   Fine grits ground.   Hulls ground.

Flour No. 2.   Dust.   Flour No. 6.   Bran.

Dust ground.
Flour No. 1.   Black dust ground.

Flour No. 4 or 5.

Wyngaert gives the quantities of these products as—

75 per cent. of No. 0;
5 per cent. of No. 1;
7 per cent. of bran;
11 per cent. of scales or hulls;
2 per cent. of loss;

Making 100 parts of the whole.

Kick gives them as—

73 per cent. of flour, Nos. 1, 2, and 3;
7 per cent. of flour, Nos. 4 and 6;
17 per cent. of bran and dust-flour;
3 per cent. of loss.

This table exhibits the method of low milling as given by Kick. It is, however, in some localities conducted with a detail and refinement which involves a much greater consumption of power and a much increased variety of products.

122. LOW MILLING.—The scheme shown in the opposite table, as compiled by Wyngaert, represented what in Germany in 1870 was known as the American or low-milling method.

The wheat is purified, by which the foreign seeds, dirt, and blasted kernels are removed. It is then pointed, or clipped, and then, in some mills, before entering the run of crackers, or groats-run, is passed between iron cylinders, which facilitate the subsequent reduction. The product, as it issues from the cracker or groats run, has a woolly rather than a gritty feel, and the coarse bran remains in large pieces. The groats are then treated as shown in the following table:

123. The processes of purification do not vary essentially from those of the Hungarian or high-milling method.

In some of the best-appointed mills in this country, (United States,) the grits or purified middlings are conducted back and discharged into the hopper with the pointed wheat. In others, the grits, which are produced in the process of half-high milling to the extent of 20 per cent. or more of the weight of the whole wheat, are ground separately, and then mixed with the residual 50 to 60 per cent. flour, in such proportions as may be determined, to give a flour of special excellence, indicated by the brand.

124. There is grown, in the State of Minnesota, a variety of spring-wheat, known as the "Fife" wheat. The berry is small, red, plump, and hard. It is distinguished on account of the extent to which the outer true bran-coat may be separated in the preliminary process of milling, without abrading the gluten-coat.

The following scheme shows the steps of the milling process as pursued in a first-class mill employing this variety of wheat:

BOLT.—*a*, Grading bolt; *b*, Groats bolt; *c*, I. Grits bolt; *d*, II. Grits bolt; *e*, III. Grits bolt; *f*, IV. Grits bolt; *g*, V. Grits bolt; *h*, Hull bolt; *i*, Hull grits bolt.

PRODUCTS OF HIGH MILLING. 57

```
                        Commercial wheat.
                            Separator.
        ┌───────────────────────┴───────────────────────┐
   Purified wheat.                                 Chicken-feed.
        │
   Smut-machine.
   ┌────┴────────────────────────┐
   Clipped wheat.           Dust, hairs, &c.
        │   between
   Scouring-brush and stone and blower.
   ┌────┴─────────────┐
   Unbranned wheat.            Scales of true bran,
        │                      longitudinal and
   First run of stones.        transverse cells,
        │                      (cigar-coat.)
   Wheat-meal.
   ┌────┴────────────────┐
   Bran.            Middlings and flour.
                            │
                  ┌─────────┴──────────┐
              Purified middlings.   Refuse sold as feed,
                    │                 b u t  containing
              First grinding.         much grits.
        ┌───────┴─────────┐
        Second middlings—flour.
              │
        Second grinding.
              │
        Best middlings flour.
```

The best middlings flour is about 25 per cent. of the wheat. The remaining flour is about 50 per cent., not so rich in gluten, but of excellent quality.

125. HIGH MILLING.—In the process of high milling, it will be remembered that in the step by step reduction of the grain, starting with the pointed kernels, we have with each grinding three products: coarse fragments, with much bran attached; less coarse fragments, with less bran attached; and minute fragments, with little or no bran attached. These are separated from each other by the sifting and purifying machines. Each of the several products is again subjected to grinding, and the product in each case again sorted into grades, and so on, until the last traces of the white interior of the berry have been separated from the dark hull and graded.

126. The following scheme exhibits the products yielded in a comparatively primitive high-milling establishment, where the details are very much less extended than in the larger and more perfect Austro-Hungarian mills, in which the processes are carried out to the last degree of refinement.

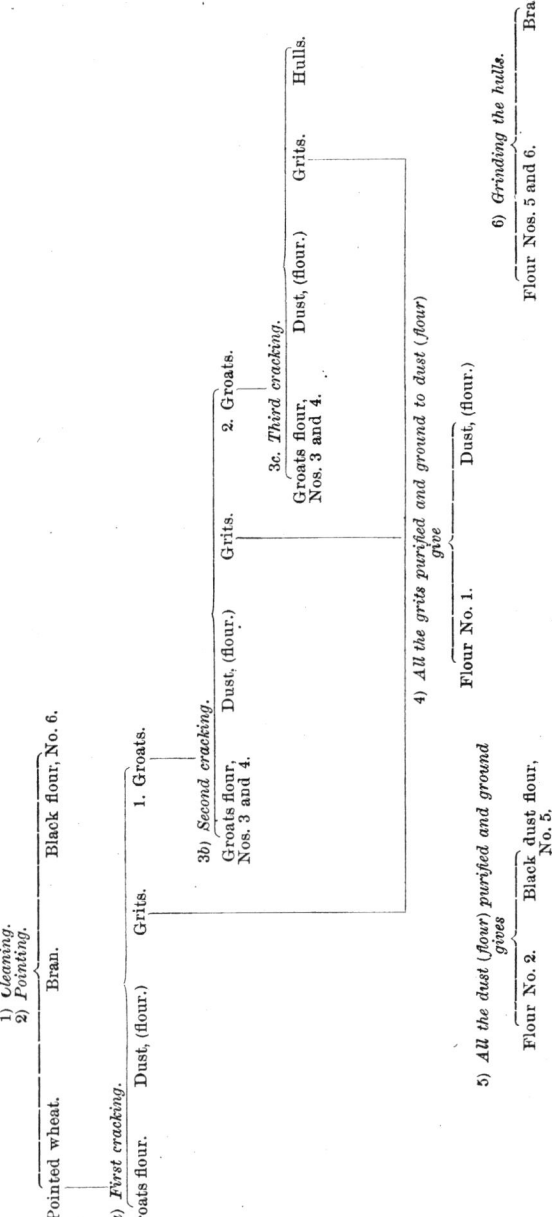

COMPREHENSIVE TABLE OF THE HUNGARIAN OR AUSTRIAN HIGH-MILLING PROCESSES.

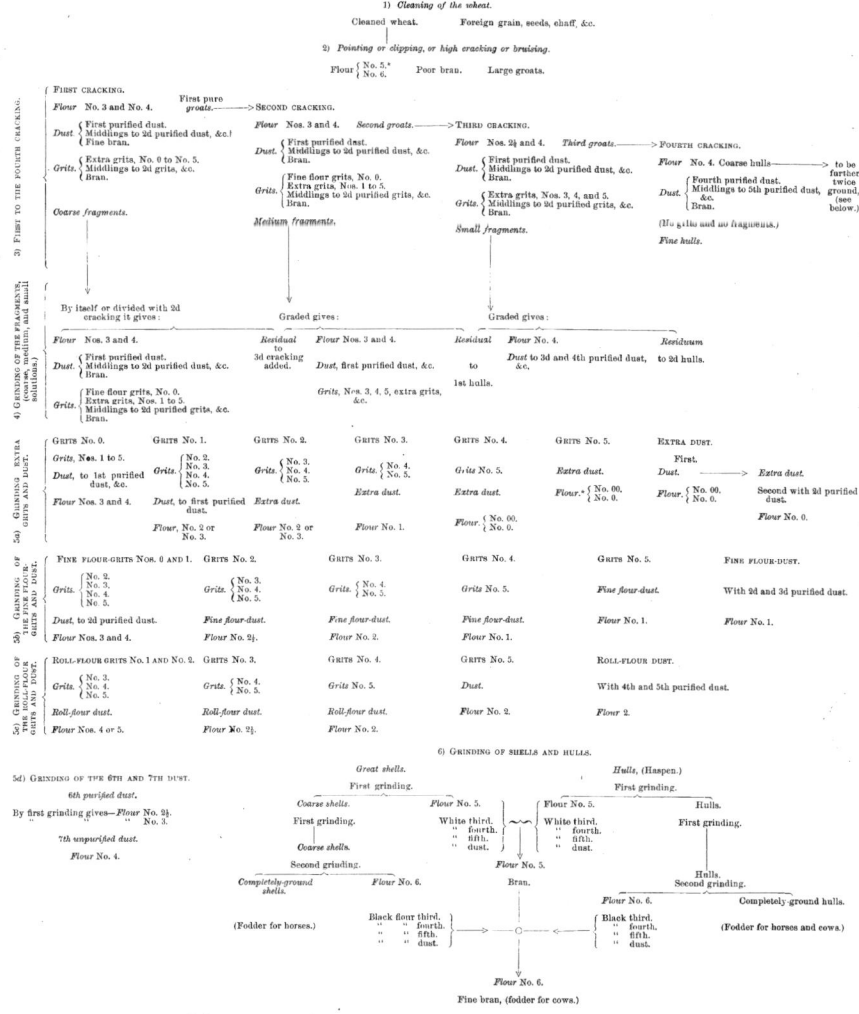

PRODUCTS OF HIGH MILLING. 59

In such a mill, the fine extract flour of grades Nos. 00 and 0 will not be obtained at all. Kick expresses a doubt whether the product thus obtained is superior to that of a well-appointed low-milling arrangement.

127. In the accompanying table, there are given the successive steps of the various processes by which wheat is milled in a thoroughly-appointed Hungarian mill.

To a layman like the writer, such a scheme seems almost bewildering in its repetition and detail, in its division and distribution of products, and their final collection and gradation. It is to be remembered, however, that the movement of the various products by means of horizontal transferring screw-work, in connection with elevators, shoots, and switches, becomes a mere matter of power in the engine.

128. It is to the circumstance of the comparatively recent development of the high-milling process in Southern Germany that the designation by numbers is not a more absolute guide in determining the actual value of the grades of flour to which these numbers are attached. Bakers were accustomed to speak of the products of the Austrian or Hungarian high milling as being of ten grades; but, in the products of the Hungarian *Walzmühle* at the Exposition, there were altogether twelve, including the groats and two grades of bran; while in the mills at Debreczin, already referred to, the subdivision was greater still.

129. In deciding upon the relative excellence of the products of the different mills submitted to the International Jury, the comparison was made, as already stated, with the best 45 per cent. of the product. This included, in the Debreczin mills, the three grades of grits, the 0 grade of flour, and the first five numbers. These were distributed as follows:

	Per cent.
A, B, C grits, and flour No. 0	6
Flour No. 1	6
Flour No. 2	6
Flour No. 3	7
Flour No. 4	9
Flour No. 5	11
	45

The remaining grades were as follows:

	Per cent.
Flour No. 6	12.0
Flour No. 7	10.0
Flour No. 8	8.0
Foot-flour No. 9	1.0
Flour No. 10	0.5
II.	
Bran	20.0
Dust	0.5
Evaporated	3.0

In the products of the Hungarian mills in Prague, the 45 per cent. includes:

	Per cent.
Flour No. 00 } Flour No. 0 }	18.9
Flour No. 1	13.8
Flour No. 2	8.6
Flour No. 2½	4.5
	45.8

130. It is obvious that for commercial purposes, where the grades making up the best 45 per cent. are to be mixed together, the finer graduation would not be recognized, and as a matter of practice the flour used for the Kaiser *Semmel* or Imperial rolls in the Vienna bakery at the Exposition rarely fell much below the best 45 per cent. of high-milled Hungarian wheat. It is from this 45 per cent., or from more or less of the higher grades included in it, that the famous Vienna bread is made.

131. The names or numbers and the percentages corresponding to these numbers as produced at the Prague high-milling establishment are:

Flour No. 00, imperial extra.
Flour No. 0, extra flour.
Flour No. 1, } baker's extra or fine flour.
Flour No. 2, }
Flour No. 3, fine flour.
Flour No. 4, roll-flour.
Flour No. 5, white pollen.
Flour No. 6, black pollen or bran and foot-flour or sweepings together.

Wyngaert, in "*Die Mühle*," No. 36, 1870, gives the following proportions of the different products yielded by the Hungarian high-milling process, which, it will be seen, are apparently inferior to the results obtained at the Debreczin mills.

	There were produced—	From wheat of average weight.	
		83 to 84 pounds per metze.	87 to 88 pounds per metze.
		Per cent.	Per cent.
A	Lady-groats		
B	Table-groats, fine	4.25	5.00
C	Table-groats, coarse		
0	Extra imperial flour		
I	Extra fine flour	5.53	5.75
II	Ordinary fine flour	5.76	6.25
III	Extra roll or semmel flour	5.51	6.75
IV	Common roll or semmel flour	6.48	7.75
V	First pollen flour	7.12	7.50
VI	Second pollen flour	13.30	15.00
VII	First dust-flour	11.85	11.00
VIII	Second dust-flour	9.95	8.75
IX	Brown pollen flour	4.36	2.25
X	Foot-flour	6.32	4.25
F	Fine bran	8.94	9.40
G	Coarse bran	6.87	7.25
H	Chicken-feed, loss, and dirt	3.76	3.10
		100.00	100.00

CYLINDER MILLS.

According to this, there would be an average produced from 100 pounds of wheat of from 34 to 39 per cent. of the better grades of flour.

132. From a comparison of these two tables with that of the Prague Hungarian mill, given by Kick and presented below, it will be seen that the numbers afford at the best but an imperfect guide. The Prague and Debreczin mills yield 45 per cent. of the choicer grades, while the results of the mills cited by Wyngaert give an average, as shown above, of 34 to 39 per cent.

Flour No. 00, imperial extra }	18.9 }
Flour No. 0, extra }	
Flour No. 1, baker's extra	13.8 } 45.8
Flour No. 2, baker's extra	8.6
Flour No. 2½, baker's extra	4.5 }
Flour No. 3, fine flour	12.6
Flour No. 4, roll or semmel flour	11.9
Flour No. 5, white pollen	7.3
Flour No. 6, black pollen	4.5
Bran and sweepings	16.4
	98.5

133. BUCHHOLZ CYLINDER-MILLS.—There has appeared in England a combination of the grinding and bolting processes of great apparent

Fig. 51.

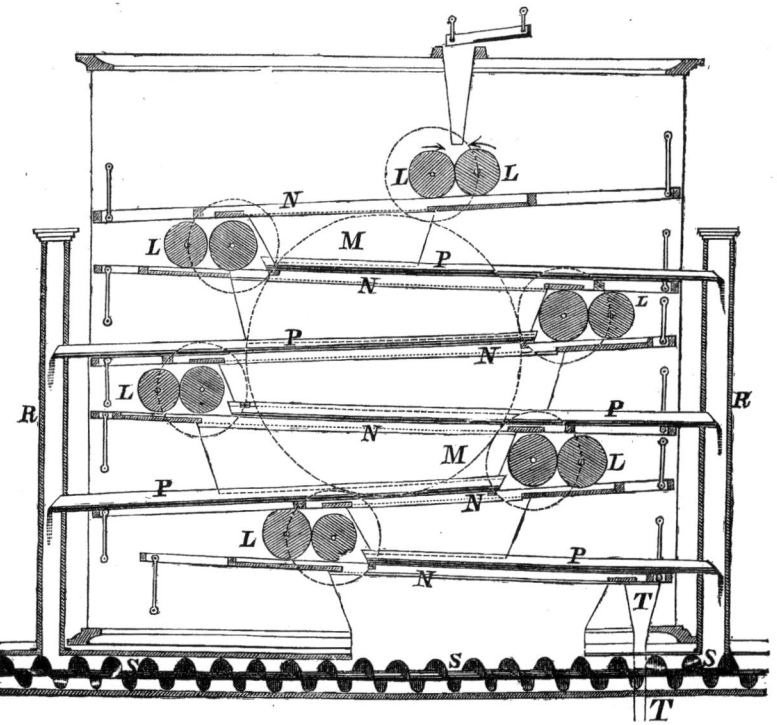

simplicity, which may properly claim a place in this connection. It is shown in section in Fig. 51 and from the end in Fig. 52.

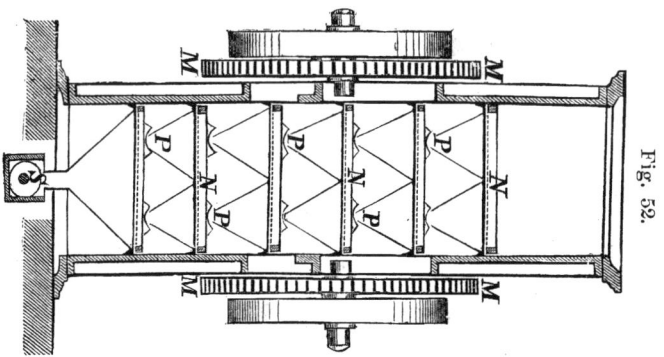

Fig. 53 exhibits a pair of cylinders one-twelfth of the actual size.

Fig. 53.

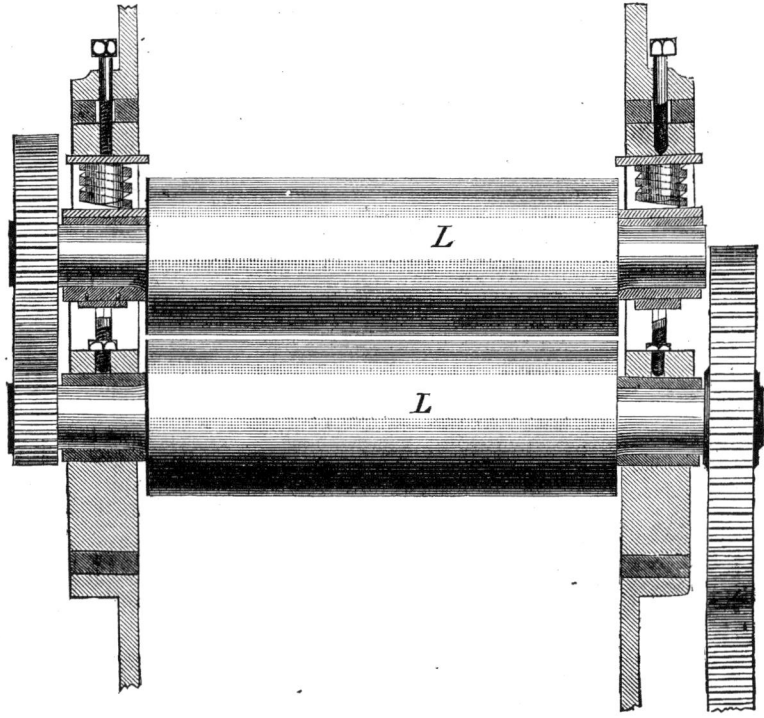

Fig. 54 is a centrifugal apparatus for grading the grits after the separation of the fine flour by the process of bolting.

The cylinders revolve with unequal velocity, and are all set in motion by a single large cog-wheel, M M. The pointed and purified grain is fed in between the highest pair of rollers L L, to be cracked as it passes through into coarse fragments, and more or less flour, grits, and bran, which are received upon the inclined shaking-sieve N, where they are sorted; the grits and fine flour passing through to the trough P, to be discharged into the upright receiver R. The groats and bran pass on to the next pair of rollers, to be further reduced to finer groats, grits, flour, and bran. Falling upon the second sieve, the flour and grits pass through to the trough P, while the bran and groats pass on to the next pair of rollers, and so on until the groats having been reduced to grits and flour, all the bran is collected in T T, and all the flour and grits in S S. The screw conducts the flour and grits to a bolt, where the flour is bolted off, and the remaining grits graded in the centrifugal machine shown in Fig. 54.

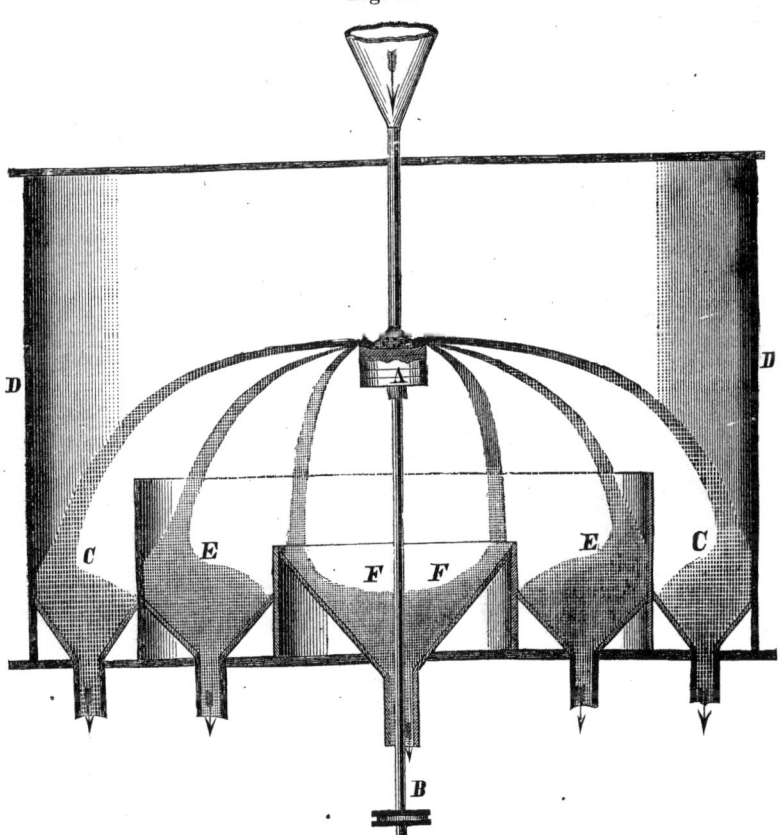

Fig. 54.

134. The average production of the Hungarian mills on exhibition at the International Exposition at Vienna gave, according to the report of van den Wyngaert and Dr. Thiel, jurors from the German empire, the following results:

	Per cent.
Flour No. 0	6.2
Flour No. 1	7.8
Flour No. 2	6.3
Flour No. 3	5.0
Flour No. 4	5.0
Flour No. 5	5.0
Flour No. 6	16.5
Flour No. 7	11.9
Flour No. 8	9.4
Flour No. 9	2.2
Fine bran	9.1
Coarse bran	11.2
Chicken-feed	0.4
Dirt and vapor	4.0
	100.0

135. THE LOW MILLING.—The following table presents the results obtained by the low-milling process in North Germany, submitted for comparison at the Exposition:

Name of the product.	1	2	3
	Per cent.	Per cent.	Per cent.
Flour No. 0	65.0 ⎫	65.0 ⎫	75.05 ⎫
Flour No. 1	6.0 ⎬ 74	8.0 ⎬ 80	4.90 ⎬ 79.95
Flour No. 2	3.0 ⎭	7.0 ⎭	.00 ⎭
Pollen flour	2.5 ⎫	⎫	⎫
Coarse or groats bran	3.0 ⎬ 21	···· ⎬ 18	6.70 ⎬ 17.85
Fine bran	···· ⎭	12.5 ⎭	···· ⎭
Coarse bran, with hull	15.5	5.5	11.15
Loss	5.0	2.0	2.20

The following table exhibits the average results of the high-milling process as obtained from wheat of high order of excellence (from 86 to 87 pounds per metze) in the Vienna mills:

	Per cent.
Flour No. 0	4
Flour No. 1	20
Flour No. 2	10
Flour No. 3	12
Flour No. 4	12
Flour No. 5	12
Flour No. 6	6
Offal, (bran)	20
Dust	4

As contrasted with this, the high-milling process yielded to C. Genz, Heidelberg, the following products:

PRODUCTS OF LOW MILLING. 65

	Per cent.
Flour No. 0	25.5
Flour No. 1	15.5
Flour No. 2	5.0
Flour No. 3	25.0
Flour No. 4	3.5
Flour No. 5	1.5
Flour No. 6	1.5
Fine bran	11.0
Coarse bran	8.0
Cockle	0.5
Waste and loss	3.0

And the following were obtained by C. Hedrich, in Glauchau, Saxony:

	Per cent.
Extra imperial flour	23.3
Flour No. 00	5.6
Flour No. 0	5.8
Flour No. 1	8.3
Flour No. 2	11.2
Flour No. 3	15.0
Overflow	2.1
Groats bran	0.8
Fine bran	8.0
Coarse bran	10.1
Clippings bran	1.7
Waste	3.9
Vapor and loss	4.2

136. In view of the foregoing tables of results, the necessity of a congress of millers for the purpose of devising, for universal adoption, systems of numbers qualifying the grades of flour, each number having a definite qualitative signification, is self-evident. The numbers in each system of milling, high, half-high, or low, should manifestly admit of simplification and greater precision of meaning.

137. Without attempting to go further into the practical details of the high-milling processes as practiced in Austro-Hungary, we may see that the object to be gained in the alternate slow reduction of the grain and its grading and cleaning is to effect the utmost possible separation of the bran, the objectionable colored part of the grain, from the white interior, and to effect this by so slight production of heat that no deterioration of flour will take place in the process. The flour produced by the high-milling process, as a necessary result of the numerous boltings and siftings, is again and again exposed to the air, and will have the

5 V B

dryness due to the climate of the region. This will necessarily prolong the period during which, without artificial drying, it may be kept without deterioration.

138. AMERICAN IMPROVED MODES.—Within the last three or four years, great improvements have been made in the better class of American mills, including the purification of commercial wheat, the adoption of the principles of the half-high milling, the *Walzmühle* or cylinder grinding, and numerous improved devices for purifying the connell or middlings. A system introduced from France two or three years since, in which the rate of revolution of the stones is greatly reduced, is specially suited to our northwestern spring-wheat, and is said to increase the yield of merchantable flour by 8 per cent.

Our method of packing in barrels is commended by German writers, although the Hungarian flour is, in general, transported in sacks. As has already been mentioned, it does not require artificial drying in order to "keep," as would be required if the grains were moistened preliminary to grinding, or as the plump, white, softer berry of the less favorable climates than that of Hungary makes necessary.

139. The flour that has uniformly stood first in our eastern markets, certainly until within a very few years, was the so-called southern flour. The wheat from which it was made was southern wheat, and was earlier in the market. The kernel was flinty and slightly shrunken. Some brands could be shipped with safety on long voyages. One of the best in repute was packed in barrels, hot, as it came from the bolt, while other flour, in the best class of mills, was uniformly cooled in the open air before packing. The brand that enjoyed this high repute, on analysis yielded at 212° Fahrenheit only 8 per cent. of water, while ordinary flours gave from 12 to 16 per cent. The latter became sour and musty when kept for long periods. The former experienced no deterioration. The reason is probably this: the heat consequent upon friction in grinding the choice brand had driven out from one-quarter to one-half of the water removable at 212° Fahrenheit; some of it water of hydration, from the gluten. This reduction in the quantity of water lessened the mobility of the molecules of the gluten, and with it, the capacity to undergo incipient fermentation. In this dried condition, the flour was packed in barrels, and the air and its moisture excluded. It was permitted to cool without opportunity to re-absorb moisture. In the case of ordinary flour, the cooling process of stirring in the open air, with the hopper-boy or its equivalent, gave opportunity for the water to be absorbed from the atmosphere. In the former case, the flour would keep for indefinitely long periods. In the latter case it would keep sweet but a comparatively short time. In the former case, the barrel of flour of 196 pounds, packed while hot, was the equivalent when fresh of from 204 to 212 pounds of flour packed after cooling in the open air. For immediate consumption, the difference in value was from 4 to 8 per

cent. in favor of the flour packed without cooling. For shipping purposes, the difference in value was of course much larger.

140. The appointments in some American mills are so complete as to enable the miller to extract the sound grains of wheat from the most varied mixtures with foreign seeds and impurities. For example, a sample of wheat obtained in the corn-market may contain sound wheat, sand, straw, stalks, chaff, oats, cockle, mustard, buckwheat, grass-seed, chess, corn, (maize,) blasted wheat.

141. This will be first passed through an inclined, revolving, cylindrical screen, having two grades of wire gauze. Through the first grade, the sand will escape. Through the second grade, all the remainder will drop except the corn, (maize,) and the larger bodies, like stalks and straw, which will go on to the tail of the screen.

The mass, freed from sand and the coarse matters, will then be fed in a thin cascade upon the jogging, inclined, perforated plates of the separator, already described, p. 22, which will remove the oats, chaff, and small fragments of straw on the one hand, and the mustard, cockle, grass-seed, and blasted wheat-grains on the other. Of these separators, a very inferior wheat would pass through three sets; then through three smut-machines with beaters, and a fourth provided with brushes; and then through a fourth separator, to remove the fine fragments, the headings and pointings produced in the smut-machines. Then follows a duster. Next the product of purified and pointed wheat passes to the run of stones, where a single grinding reduces the whole to meal. In the mill specially examined, the stones were 52 inches in diameter, having logarithmic, spiral furrows $\frac{3}{16}$ to $\frac{1}{4}$ of an inch deep, with finely-grooved, alternating lands of about equal area, the leading furrows running to the eye of the stone numbering 22, alternating with 22 short furrows running into the leading furrows. From the stones, the meal issues at a temperature of about 120° Fahrenheit, and is conducted to the bolts, where the first fine flour is separated from the remainder of bran, middlings, feed, tailings, &c., which are afterward graded by bolting.

142. The finer bran of the middlings, after passing through the middlings-purifier described on p. 52, goes into the "feed." The coarse bran goes to the bran-duster. The white interior, having been detached from the hulls, is conducted back to re-enter the whole meal on its way to the bolts. The middlings (grits) may be ground separately or discharged with the purified and pointed wheat directly into the run of stones.

The running stones make about 170 revolutions per minute; the bran-dusters, about 450 revolutions; and the smut-machines, about 500 in the same time.

The above is an outline of the processes observed in Jewells Brothers' mills at Brooklyn, N. Y.

143. CHARACTERISTICS OF FLOUR.—The best wheat flour has a faint, pleasant aroma; is dry, heavy, by transmitted light having a light shade of clear brilliant-yellow, and readily balls in the hand. An inferior article, when pressed in the hand, shows a quality of adhesion, retaining the form imparted by the pressure.

Under the microscope, cells of larger and lesser size are readily recognized, and also the still lesser cells of albuminoid bodies, which, unlike the starch-cells, are not colored with iodine, and also portions of the frame-work of the cellular tissue of the interior, in which the starch and albuminoid cells are lodged.

144. Dr. Julius Wiesner, professor in the University of Vienna, of the international jury Group IV, in an elaborate paper upon the morphology of wheat-starch, recognizes three kinds of starch-granules, under the names of the lenticular, the small spherical or polyhedric, and the compound grains. The last variety had not been recognized by previous observers. They are found in the interior of the gluten-coat, and are made up of from two to twenty-five individual granules. These compound grains are rarely found in commercial starch, and seldom otherwise than in broken fragments. In admeasurements, the greater number of the grains showed two very unlike magnitudes, the one of the large lens-shaped, and the other of the smaller grain.

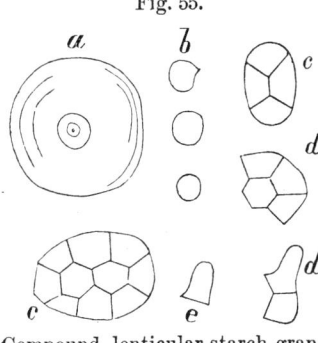

Fig. 55.

Compound lenticular starch-granules, (Wiesner.)

145. The accompanying diagram (Fig. 55) exhibits the different forms under a magnifying power of 1,000: a, the large lenticular simple starch-grain; b, the small simple starch-grain; cc, the compound starch-grain; dd, fragments of the compound starch-grain; e, the fragment of a twin starch-grain. The diameters of the large lenticular starch-grains are given in the following schedule:

Varieties.	Least diameter.	Greatest diameter.	Most frequent diameter.
	Millimeters.	Millimeters.	Millimeters.
Triticum vulgare (1)	0.0140	0.0390	0.0282
Triticum durum (2)	0.0110	0.0360	0.0261
Triticum turgidum (3)	0.0176	0.0411	0.0290
Triticum spelta (4)	0.0154	0.0396	0.0270
Triticum dicoccum (5)	0.0111	0.0301	0.0259
Triticum monococcum (6)	0.0120	0.0270	0.0195

(1) Twenty-three varieties from Mähren, Hungary, France, Italy, Chili, and Victoria (Australia) were examined.
(2) Six varieties from Mähren, Hungary, France, and Algiers.
(3) Fifteen varieties from Mähren, Lower Austria, Hungary, Switzerland, England, East India, Chili, and New South Wales.
(4) Four varieties from Würtemberg and Baden.
(5) Two varieties from the Vienna collection; origin unknown.
(6) Three varieties from the Vienna collection; origin unknown.

CHARACTERISTICS OF FLOUR.

The same varieties of wheat that were employed in the determination of the magnitude of these granules served for the measure of the small starch-granules.

The small starch-granules gave the following magnitudes:

Varieties.	Least diameter.	Greatest diameter.	Most frequent diameter.
	Millimeters.	Millimeters.	Millimeters.
Triticum vulgare	0.0022	0.0082	0.0072
Triticum durum	0.0022	0.0078	0.0072
Triticum turgidum	0.0025	0.0082	0.0072
Triticum spelta	0.0025	0.0079	0.0070
Triticum dicoccum	0.0018	0.0068	0.0066
Triticum monococcum	0.0018	0.0060	0.0058

146. The compound starch-grains are found in the outer as well as inner layers of the gluten-coat; more frequently, however, in the inner layer. The quantity of these grains in comparison with the larger and lenticular grain is not large, the general form is elliptic or egg-shape, and they frequently exceed in size the large lenticular starch-grains. The largest of the compound grains measured by Dr. Wiesner had a diameter of 0.0324 millimeter. It is easy to distinguish under the microscope between wheat-starch and the various other starches in commerce, by their size, forms, and markings, with the exception of the starch of rye and of barley.

In Fig. 56 are rye-starch grains, magnified 750 times; and in the next figure, 57, we have the starch-grains of barley, magnified 750 times. The difficulty arises from the circumstance that the starch-granules in the seed are found alike in the gluten-coat of the wheat, rye, and barley, and are of substantially the same size.

In the wheat-grain that has begun to grow, the starch-grains present the appearance given in the following diagram, (Fig. 58.)

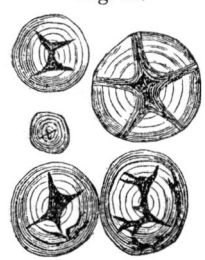

Fig. 58.

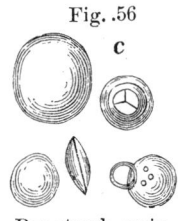

Fig. 56.

Rye starch-grain.

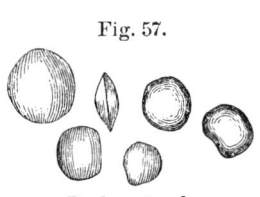

Fig. 57.

Barley-starch.

Starch-growing wheat.

Lesser fissures than those shown in the cut are also sometimes to be observed in the starch-grains of perfectly sound wheat.

147. GLUTEN-CELLS.—On page 4, we have a cross-section of the coats of the wheat upon a scale of four hundred diameters.

In the accompanying diagram, (59,) we have the ripe barley-grain on a cale of three hundred diameters. It will be remarked that the gluten-coat presents from two to three and even more layers of cells.

In the following figure, (60,) we have a section of the oat-grain.

In Fig. 61, we have a section of rice.

In Fig. 62, we have a section of Indian corn; and in Fig. 63, a section of rye.

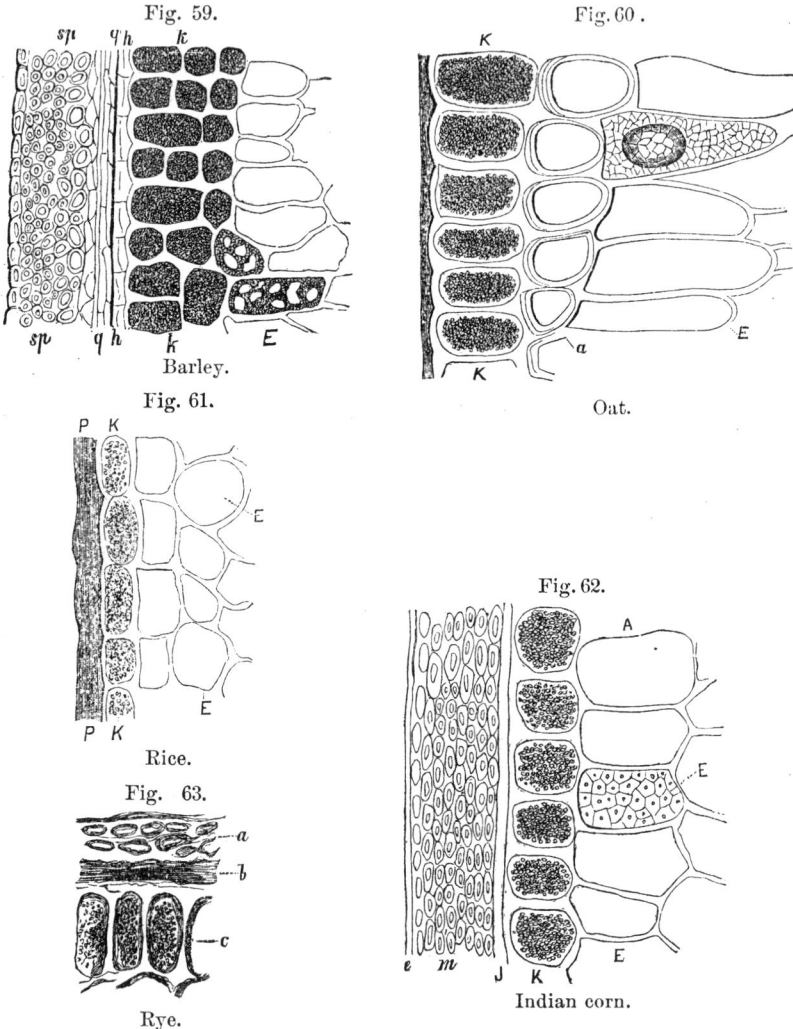

Fig. 59. Barley.
Fig. 60. Oat.
Fig. 61. Rice.
Fig. 62. Indian corn.
Fig. 63. Rye.

148. Upon comparing these sections with each other, it will be seen that the structure of the different grains that have served from time immemorial as the material for the supply of farinaceous food of the world, has certain great distinguishing characteristics.

Within a series of layers of woody fiber, serving for the protection of the nutritious interior, and otherwise com aratively worthless, we have one or more layers of cells, containing the nitrogenous compounds and phosphatic salts, which serve the most important purposes of nutrition, as they largely furnish the materials for the various tissues of the human organism; and within these layers, to the center of the grain, a mass of starch-granules, larger and lesser, and cells containing albumi noids, supported in a loose frame-work of cellular tissue.

149. The art of milling in its perfection consists in the *disintegration*, not *destruction*, of these tissues and cells, and the removal from them of the woody fiber. This is more perfectly accomplished in the milling of the wheat than in that of any of the other grains, with perhaps the exception of the rice, and yields the whitest and to the palate the most acceptable flour.

150. HUNGARIAN PRIZE FLOUR.—In comparing the flours of the different countries with each other, the jury, in the first place, compared with each other the best 45 per cent. of the wheat of all the products of high milling; then all the products of half-high milling were compared together, and lastly the products of low milling.

The *average* of the products of the Hungarian mills with the high milling process stood (0 being perfection) 0.015. Of these, the flour of the Pesth *Walzmühle* held the first rank. The director of the mills, Herr Dosswald, received an imperial decoration. Of this flour, I obtained the complete series, including the grits and brans. The interest that attaches to this collection led me to make an analysis, which is herewith submitted.

151. By treating 0 flour with iodine, it is easy to make every large starch-granule blue, while all the minute grains (nitrogenous bodies) remain unchanged in color. Then, by treating another portion of flour with ammonio-nitrate of silver, the minute particles (nitrogenous bodies) will become yellow, while the starch-granules remain unchanged in color. This latter experiment proves at the same time the presence in the nitrogenous bodies of phosphoric acid, indeed of phosphates.

The No. 0 Hungarian flour has, under the microscope, a cleaner look, is freer from fine particles (of the albuminoid bodies?) than the product of low or half-high milling, as shown in the best grades of western flour in the Boston market. The mode of grading pursued at the Pesth mill would separate the finest particles; and as these are chiefly the little granules corresponding in appearance with those in the gluten-sacs of the inner shell, it is at once explained why the nitrogen should be less in the zero flour of Hungary.

		Water.	Ash.	Phosphoric acid.	Nitrogen.	Albuminoids, estimated from the nitrogen.
Grits	A	10.57	0.44	0.24	2.25	14.65
Imperial selection, or extra	No. 0	10.37	0.42	0.14	1.68	10.76
	No. 1	10.23	0.46	0.21	1.68	10.76
	No. 2	10.47	1.03	0.22	1.72	11.02
	No. 3	10.07	1.02	0.17	1.72	11.02
Semmel-flour, or roll-flour	No. 4	10.24	1.19	0.25	1.74	11.15
	No. 5	9.66	0.61	0.35	1.80	11.54
Bread-flour	No. 6	11.12	1.04	0.24	1.84	11.79
	No. 7	10.99	0.81	0.21	1.80	11.54
Black flour	No. 8	9.86	1.01	0.36	1.90	12.18
Fine bran	No. 9	9.71	7.32	2.96	1.98	12.69
Coarse bran	No. 10	11.01	4.21	1.74	2.21	14.16

152. These results will be intelligible if we understand that in the main the numbers may be regarded as qualifying the composition of the berry as one goes outward from the core to the surface of the unbrauned or clipped grain. The grits are coarse fragments of the interior, carrying with them more or less of the gluten-coat, from which the true bran has been removed.

It will be remarked that the ash, or mineral portion, increases from the core to the surface; and that the phosphoric acid obeys the same law, though the rates are not the same. The nitrogen, as representing the total albuminoid bodies, also increases except in the grits, (A,) and in that the nitrogen is in marked excess.

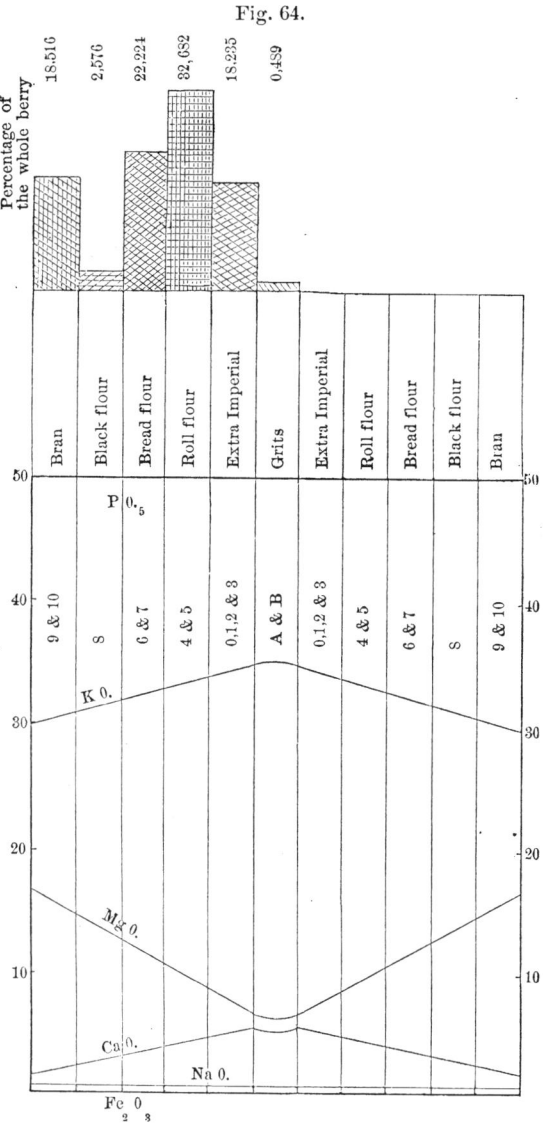

Fig. 64.

HUNGARIAN PRIZE FLOUR.

153. Dempwolff made, at the instance of the late Baron Liebig, an elaborate analysis of the products of the Hungarian *Walzmühlen*, which I add in an appendix.

One of the striking results of Dempwolff's analysis I have illustrated in the foregoing cut, (Fig. 64.) He found the phosphoric acid to be about 50 per cent. of the ash in every part of the berry. The oxide of iron and the soda were each present in small quantity, and each in its constant percentage of the ash in all parts of the berry. The lime and potassa, however, increased from without inward—from the surface toward the core—while the magnesia diminished.

154. The cut also exhibits the relative total weights of the different products in percentages, indicated by volumes.

155. The white body of the interior of the berry is, for the most part, a mass of starch-grains of sizes, according to Prof. Julius Wiesner, ranging in diameter from 0.0110 to 0.0410 millimeter; or an average of about the one-thousandth of an inch. Embedded in this mass of starch are clusters of cells of a diameter ranging from 0.0022 to 0.0082 millimeter, or an average of two ten-thousandths of an inch in diameter, and containing nitrogen in their composition. These cells are the depositaries of the albuminoid bodies and the mineral constituents found in the interior of the berry. Among these smaller cells are also small starch-granules. On crushing a lump of the grits and placing it under a microscope, the starch-granules are seen surrounded by a great profusion of these albuminoid cells. As compared with No. 0 flour, the relative proportion of starch-granules in the latter is vastly greater. It would seem, therefore, that the cohesion of the mass in a lump of grits is a coincident fact, if it be not due largely, to the presence in it of the albuminoid bodies.

156. The composition of the 0 flour and the A grits is indicated in the following figures:

	A grits.	0 flour.
Ash	0.44	0.43
Phosphoric acid	0.24	0.14
Nitrogen	2.25	1.68

Occasional lumps of the grits are seen to have still adhering to them the gluten-coat, and even portions of the outer bran-coat. The presence of phosphoric acid in the minute grains of the interior of the grits may be readily shown by immersing the crushed grits in a solution of ammonio-nitrate of silver. The minute albuminoid cells become yellow, as already shown, from the formation of tribasic phosphate of silver, and are quite readily distinguished from the minute starch-grains.

157. In comparing this flour No. 0 with ordinary low-milled flour, under the microscope, one remarks a striking uniformity in size among the particles of the latter. One also remarks relatively very few broken or bruised starch-grains in the high-milled flour, while the reverse is true of the low-milled flour.

158. It would seem that the grits are due to the presence, in the particular mass of starch-grains and frame-work of cellular tissue, of some agglutinating material binding the grains and tissue together. Under the microscope, this material is seen in clusters of minute cells embedded in the mass of starch, and corresponding in size with the minute cells that fill the gluten-sacs. If a grits-fragment be moistened, and subjected to pressure upon a glass slide, and the upper thin glass plate be moved about, the tenacity and elasticity of the material of the albuminoid cells may be readily discerned. This is in keeping with the greater measure of gluten and the larger percentage of nitrogen in the grits as compared with that in the finer grades of flour.

This explanation of the nature and cause of the grits, as produced by the process of high or half-high milling, is in keeping with the climatic conditions which make a flinty wheat—that is, which cause a more rapid exhalation of moisture and an arrest of movement of the nitrogenous constituents toward the periphery of the berry. The flour-granules—that is, the finer portions resulting from abrasion of the grits—contain less gluten than the grits, for the obvious reason that, had they contained more gluten, they would have been less readily reduced to powder.

159. MODE OF TESTING FLOUR.—This belongs to the class of unwritten arts. To the inexperienced eye, all grades of flour, except the very worst, appear white, when each is examined by itself. When, however, several samples are placed side by side, and their surfaces made smooth by drawing over them lightly a polished spatula, they are seen to differ from each other in color, and especially if the samples be placed upon blue paper. The shade of yellowness will be seen to be due in some instances, as a magnifying-glass of moderate power will show, to minute particles of the interior bran still adhering to small grits; to fragments of the color-coat, especially the portion in the groove of the berry; or to fragments of the embryo. It may also be due to the actual color of the interior of some varieties of slightly-shrunken, hard, or flinty grain, which, when cut with a knife, presents, in the cross-section, a shade of pale reddish-yellow.

Any blue shade which the flour may present will be due to the minute fragments of the hulls of black foreign seeds, or possibly to particles of smut.

The feeling of grit in the flour, to be determined by rubbing between the thumb and finger, is one of the qualities in which flours from grains of unequal hardness differ from each other.

160. The aroma of the flour of recently-ground, fresh, sound grain is grateful to the sense of smell. But if the flour be old, and especially if it has not been adequately dried, or has been made from wheat "grown," or sprouted, in the shock, or has been subjected to excessive heat in the process of grinding, it will exhale products of fermentation that are more or less offensive.

161. If a small sample of flour be moistened with half its weight of water, and wrought into dough with the thumb and finger, it will exhibit the degree of tenacity and elasticity and a certain quality of liveliness, as it is termed, which causes it to return to its original form when extended or indented, upon which the baker depends to make his bread porous.

If the gluten, of which this tenacity is the normal property, be greatly deteriorated, the dough will "run," and the inferiority of the flour for those purposes which depend upon the tenacity and elasticity of the gluten will be proportioned substantially to the facility with which the dough "runs." This softening of the gluten points to rusted wheat, or wheat grown upon fields richly manured with concentrated organic manures, or wheat deteriorated from the presence of foreign seeds, as those of wild onion, but more frequently to flour that has itself been heated, or flour produced from wheat that has been wet and not properly dried, or grown in the field after harvesting and before housing.

162. The *chemical examination* consumes more time, but also determines certain points of importance which can be ascertained in no other way. The percentage determination of the nitrogen has been shown, by the researches of Krocker and Horsford, (Liebig's *Annalen*,) to be sufficient to determine at once with great precision the percentage, on the one hand of the gluten and associated albuminoid bodies, and on the other the starch with its small quantities of dextrine and sugar. The determination of the ash by burning, points at once to the percentage of nutritive mineral matter, as the phosphates for example; and the determination of the water which may be driven out at 212° points to the susceptibility of the flour to spontaneous deterioration. The larger the percentage of moisture present the less likely is the wheat to keep. The determination of the starch and gluten by subjecting a weighed quantity of flour moistened and fashioned into a ball of dough to a slender stream of water will yield a trustworthy result for the starch, but only for the gluten of perfectly sound flour; and even in that the vegetable albumen, caseine, and cerealine of Mége Mouriès will be more or less dissolved and lost.

163. The whole of the nitrogenous bodies may be separated from the starch by treatment with diluted acetic acid, and, after the settling-out of the starch, the determination of the specific gravity of the solution will give the amount of the nitrogenous constituents.

HUNGARIAN MILL INDUSTRIES.

164. In the pamphlet accompanying the collective exhibition of the product of milling of Buda-Pesth and the cities of five Hungarian provinces, it is stated that the products of the wheat are exhibited in one kind of grits, nine sorts (No. 0–8) of flour, and two kinds of bran, (coarse and fine.) The Hungarian mill-industry is based in general on the total cereal production of the Hungarian kingdom, but especially

on the quality of the Hungarian wheat. Besides being rich in flour of extraordinary keeping quality, it contains more gluten than other varieties of wheat. The milling-art is so conducted that, taking advantage of every improvement in rendering it more perfect, the great excellencies of the raw material are rendered appreciable and brought into service. The Hungarian flour produced by high milling is, in the points of purity, whiteness, yield and keeping qualities, not equaled by that of any other country. Its keeping quality has been illustrated under trying circumstances—in transportation by sea under the equator, where for a whole year it has yielded from every 100 pounds of flour, 160 pounds of bread, of characteristic nutritive value and excellent taste. The mills of Buda-Pesth, for the most part erected or enlarged between 1865 and 1869, cost about $5,000,000. They contain 500 run of stones, and 168 *Walz* sets (of three pairs each) of steel rollers. They have a capacity of about 1,000,000,000 pounds of wheat per annum, valued at $37,000,000.

The mills of the provinces erected between 1862 and 1872 cost about $1,250,000, have 128 run of stones, and grind about 200,000,000 pounds of grain, having a value of about $7,500,000.

165. The preceding discussion will have qualified us to appreciate the excellence of the material from which the renowned Vienna bread is made, and we proceed to the discussion of the preliminary steps to its production.

CHAPTER III.

MAKING YEAST BREAD.

166. BREAD.—Bread in its widest signification comprehends all the forms of farinaceous food which have been subjected to the processes of the culinary art. It embraces, besides loaf-bread, rolls and biscuit, the cracker, the merely boiled dough, the griddle-cake, and the numerous fanciful forms of farinaceous confectionery. For the most part, when fitted for consumption as food, they have received a cellular structure, and are light. The practical advantage of this porosity is that when eaten the digestive fluids—the saliva and gastric juice—readily penetrate the mass and promptly perform their function. The objection to "heavy" bread is that its digestion is retarded, and that is because the digestive fluids come in contact only with the outside of comparatively large masses; the absence of cellular structure preventing their penetration to the interior.

167. The superior digestibility of porous bread was known to the ancients, but, because its preparation required the use of flour already in a state of fermentation and decay, which filled the mass with bubbles and was offensive to smell and taste, it was proscribed from sacred uses on account of its conceived *impurity*. For these uses unleavened bread, which was a sort of Graham wafer, was required. This was mainly a product obtained by heating to a baking temperature a thin layer of paste made of whole meal or cracked grains and water.

The term *bread*, in its more limited signification, is applied to porous loaves and rolls. If the product contain butter or sugar, or spices or perfumes, or fruit, it is pastry, cake, or confectionery rather than bread There are exceptions to this definition. The mixed rye and wheat bread of Austro-Hungary, and the inferior roll and *Semmel* bread have sometimes, to disguise the odor or taste, a few caraway-seeds.

168. To secure the cellular structure of the bread, it is necessary that the flour should have a constituent which, when moistened with water at common temperature, shall possess two of the properties of India rubber, tenacity and elasticity ; and that these properties shall, in a great degree, be lost on subjecting the moistened flour or kneaded dough to a certain elevated temperature. This body which nature has provided in the cereals is gluten, and in wheat it is associated with a mass of starch of remarkable whiteness and purity, and yields, when properly prepared and the baking processes are properly conducted, a product

exceedingly grateful to the palate. This palatability in the best forms of bread is partly due to the changes wrought in the starch of the interior crumb, which is largely a mere physical, not a chemical, change, and the changes which take place in the starch and gluten of the exterior crust, due to incipient destructive distillation, or roasting, and partly to the absence of special or marked odor and taste in the bread as a whole.

169. FERMENTATION.—The knowledge that whole meal wet with water will go into spontaneous fermentation must have been coeval with that of the first use of leavened bread. The philosophy of the changes which the flour undergoes in fermentation is of comparatively recent study and practical development. That a small portion of flour already in process of active fermentation would, when mixed with fresh flour and water, cause it to go into more prompt fermentation than when left to spontaneous change, must also have been known at an early period. Upon this was based the practice of setting apart a portion of the dough of each batch of bread to be employed in raising the succeeding batch, and this process prevails largely over the world at this day.

170. Pure starch mixed with water experiences no decomposition, but pure gluten mixed with water and set aside in a warm place, soon begins to swell from the production of gas-bubbles in its interior, and to exhale products at first grateful but at a later period offensive to the sense of smell, and from having had at the outset qualities of tenacity and elasticity, which permitted the formation and retention of gas-bubbles, it loses its tenacity in great degree, so that its bubbles escape from the larger volume, and the porous mass collapses to a smaller volume, and the material itself becomes semi-liquid. The changes it has experienced have given to the mass an acid reaction; it has become sour; various volatile products have been formed; the permanent fluid portions have taken on new composition and new qualities. If this mass be examined with a powerful microscope, it is found to contain, besides the materials furnished directly from the flour, numerous very minute bodies, of an irregular spherical form, which have been ascertained to be capable of carrying with themselves the capacity to produce fermentation when transferred to fresh mixtures of flour and water. These little bodies are the yeast-plant. They are the minute agencies of fermentation possessed by the sour dough. They are contained in countless myriads in a cent's worth of baker's yeast. They constitute the actual value in the brewer's and distiller's yeast. They are the principal bodies which are produced by following the various recipes for making potato-yeast, hop-yeast, bran-yeast, barm, &c. They are contained pure, with the exception of water, which constitutes from 70 to 80 per cent., in the moist German press-yeast cakes. It is estimated that a single cubic inch of the air-dried press-yeast contains some 1,200,000,000 of these minute organisms.

171. The researches of Dr. Julius Wiesner have shown that the fresh

FERMENTATION.

yeast cells (that is, cells taken from a fermenting fluid) are, for the most part, spherical or slightly elliptical, rarely oval, having an average greater diameter of 0.0087 millimeter. They are sacs, as shown in Fig. 65; a containing granules, as seen in b, and are, for the most part, filled with the jelly-like protoplasm, the center of which appears more transparent from the presence of a little air-cell, or vacuole, as indicated in c; d is the jelly, or protoplasm; and e, the thin space, or vacuole. The cells increase by budding.

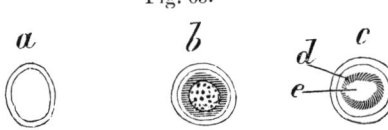

Fig. 65.

According to Pasteur, the young cells do not separate from the parent cells until they have attained to nearly the same size. According to other authors, including Mitscherlich, the yeast-cells also increase by bursting and diffusing their granular contents through the liquid; the granules then developing into cells.

172. Blondeau maintains that the young cells once separated always remain isolated, and never form branches, or elongated cells, like those that accompany lactic fermentation.

173. The following outline-diagrams (Fig. 66) illustrate the growth

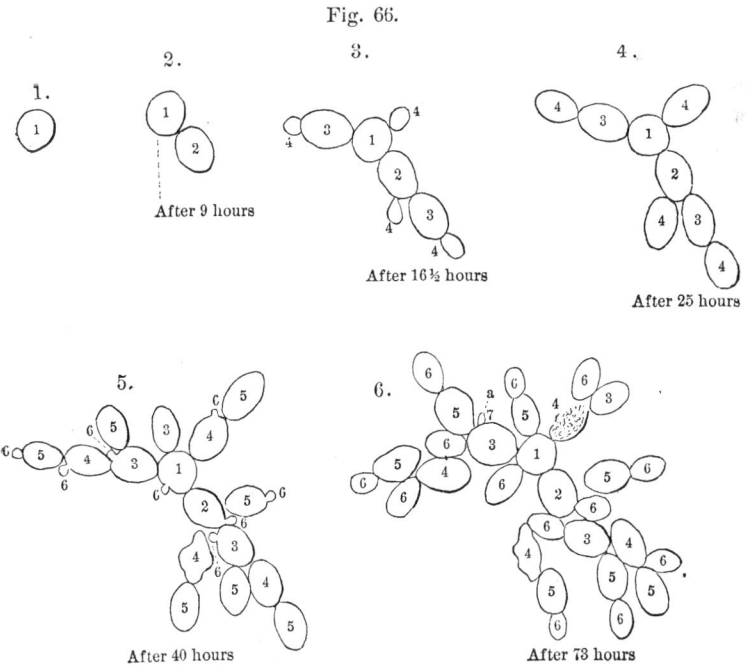

of the yeast-plant from hour to hour, as observed under the microscope by Mitscherlich, (see vol. i, p. 372, Mitscherlich's *Lehrbuch*.)

The yeast-cells were taken from the malt-extract, placed between glass plates, the edges of which were covered with melted wax to prevent evaporation, and kept at a temperature of about 66° Fahrenheit. The drawings were at intervals, as follows: 1, parent cell; 2, after 9 hours; 3, after 7½ hours more; 4, after 8½ hours more; 5, after 15 hours more; 6, after 33 hours more.

174. The younger cells not yet separated from the parent cells appear hyaline, crystalline, or extremely fine-grained. In perfectly-developed cells, one distinguishes readily the glassy, bluish plasma, (gelatinous contents of the cell,) and in the midst of it one or two, rarely three, reddish-appearing cavities having an average diameter half that of the cell. If these cells are transferred from a fermenting fluid into distilled water, they are observed immediately to swell with increase in size of their cavities. After a few days, they are enlarged to diameters occasionally as great as 0.138 millimeter; the cavities become enormously large, and sometimes fill the whole, and in elliptical cells extend from wall to wall bounding the shortest diameter. If, however, the yeast-cells are placed in a solution containing 20 per cent. or more of sugar, the cells lessen in size and by slow stages are reduced to one-half their original dimensions, and the cavities entirely disappear.

These experiments show that the cavities are increased by addition of water and reduced by its abstraction.

175. By drying the cells till they cease to lose weight—that is, first *in vacuo* and then in an air-bath at a temperature of from 230° to 248° Fahrenheit—they may be reduced to a diameter of from 0.0045 to 0.0068 millimeter, when the cavities will have entirely disappeared. They become shriveled and assume a yellowish tint. These dried cells will again take in water upon exposure with very great avidity. In a solution 10 to 15 per cent. strong of sugar, these cells become charged with numerous small reddish drops of water, having the appearance on a small scale of the larger cavities before mentioned.

Wiesner distinguishes between these cavities and the former ones as abnormal and normal cavities. The normal cavities are for the most part single, and seldom exceed three in number, while the abnormal are reddish, numerous, and spread about through the plasma of the cell.

176. Drying at a temperature of 212° Fahrenheit continued for several hours will not kill the yeast-plants, but all except the very youngest go over into the condition of abnormal cavities.

The young cells that have had no cavities will be the starting-point for fermentation, when yeast so dried is added to a solution of sugar.

The presence of numerous cavities is an evidence of impaired capacity for producing fermentation. The young undeveloped cells have no cavities except in very diluted solutions. The young full-grown cells have large cavities, and the old cells have the numerous small cavities. *All yeast-cells having cavities convert sugar into alcohol and carbonic acid.* Those having the abnormal cavities—that is, the numerous cavities— and those which have no cavities, having, first of all, either from age or any

FERMENTATION. 81

other cause, passed through the stage preceding the formation of abnormal cavities, produce no fermentation; they are dead. The young cells, though without cavities, as they develop will acquire normal *cavities*, and then will produce alcoholic fermentation. Solutions containing only from 2 to 4 per cent. and from 20 to 25 per cent. of sugar, seem most favorable to the chemical and physical conditions of fermentation. In such solutions, the fermentation is complete. Solutions containing from 12 to 13 per cent. of sugar, or above 25 per cent. of sugar, do not undergo complete fermentation. The relations therefore of concentration and dilution of solution, influencing, by endosmosis and exosmosis, the condition of the contents of the cavities of the yeast-cells, determine the best circumstances for fermentation. The relative quantities of carbonic acid, alcohol, succinic acid, butyric acid, acetic acid, formic acid, lactic acid, and glycerine which arise in the process of fermentation are evidently dependent on the relations of the water to the protoplasm of the yeast-cells, and obviously also upon the percentage of sugar or concentration of the solution.

177. The following diagrams from Enyrim exhibit various appearances of the yeast-plants as observed by him.

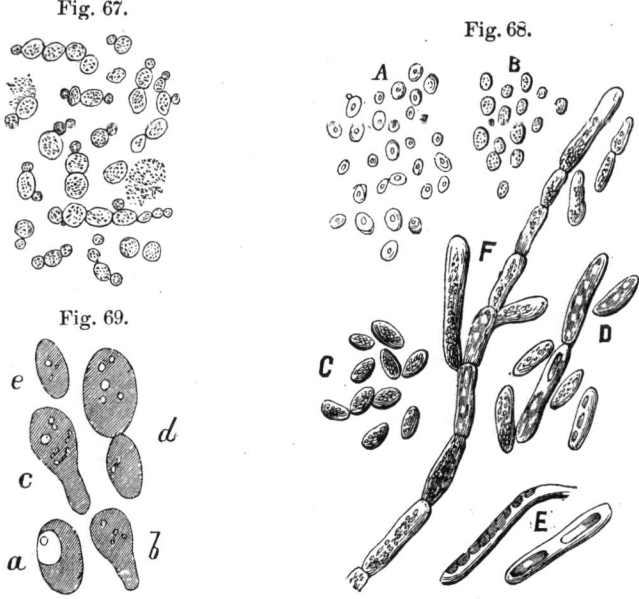

Fig. 67.

Fig. 68.

Fig. 69.

In Fig. 67, we have the appearance of yeast taken from mash, eight hours in fermentation, exhibiting the germs and the increase by budding and their union in the form of chains or threads.*

Fig. 68 exhibits the developed yeast-plant and the series of successive developments. In A, we have the cells with their cavities capable of

---
* They seem also to be charged with the abnormal cavities observed by Dr. Wiesner, and therefore incapable of alcoholic fermentation.

6 V B

producing alcoholic fermentation; in B, we probably have the cells as observed by Dr. Wiesner, containing numerous abnormal cavities no longer capable of producing alcoholic fermentation; and in C, D, E, and F, probably the yeast-plant present with the lactic fermentation. Fig. 69, which is from the upper ferment of white-beer yeast magnified a thousand-fold, illustrates, in a, the parent cell, which in b is elongated, in c still more elongated, in d resolved into two adhering cells, the parent and the bud, and in e the young cell separated from the parent bud.

178. Dr. Hassall, well known from his researches on the subject of adulteration of food, has traced the yeast-plant, as he believes, successfully through these various stages of development.

Blondeau recognized the elongated or branch cells as connected with the *lactic* fermentation.

The weighty investigation of Dr. Wiesner has shown that the only forms of yeast-cells capable of producing alcohol and carbonic acid in solutions of sugar are the nearly round cells, which, in the observation of Pasteur, are produced by budding, and remain in contact with the parent cell, to be separated only when they have attained to nearly equal size, and thereafter, according to Blondeau, maintaining their isolated condition, and which have acquired normal cavities.

179. THE THEORY OF FERMENTATION.—The theory of fermentation is not yet settled. Pasteur, the advocate of the notion that the division of sugar into alcohol and carbonic acid is a concomitant of the vital processes of the yeast-plant, and, as a consequence, that the living yeast-cell is indispensably necessary for alcoholic fermentation, has the support of Helmholz since 1844.

Pasteur has shown that if the spores of the yeast-plant (*Penicilium glaucum* or *Mycoderma vini*) be sown on the surface of a fermentable liquid, having taken care to exclude all other germs, the fungus grows and develops on the *surface* an air-plant, absorbing oxygen from the air, and giving off carbonic acid, without the production of alcohol. If the liquid be agitated, and the film submerged, for a time there is no further change; but if the proper temperature be maintained, after a while bubbles of carbonic acid are given off, and the liquid yields alcohol on distillation. According to Pasteur, whether the yeast-plant shall occasion putrefaction or vinous fermentation in a fermentable liquid—such as a solution of sugar—depends on whether the growth takes place in the air at the surface of the liquid, or within the liquid below the surface.*

---

*Pasteur cites the following experiment: "If we half fill a flask with a fermentable liquid, such as a solution of sugar, and, having taken care to exclude all other germs, sow on its surface some spores of *Mycoderma vini* or *Penicilium glaucum*, the fungus grows and flourishes on the surface, feeding on the organic matter in the solution, absorbing oxygen from the air, and throwing off carbonic-acid gas. In this case, no alcohol is produced. If we now shake the flask, the film of fungus sinks through the liquid, and for a time there is no further change; but, after resting a little, if the tem-

180. A ferment is a living body, which is special in this respect, that it is capable of performing the functions of its life apart from *free* oxygen; it can assimilate directly oxygenated matters, such as sugar, and derive from them the requisite amount of heat; and it further can produce the decomposition of a much greater weight of fermentable matter than the weight of the ferment in action. Pasteur has found that ferments, such as yeast, lose their fermenting power—that is to say, the amount of organic matter decomposed diminishes and approaches the weight of the ferment employed—exactly in proportion to the amount of the oxygen supplied.

181. Pasteur claims to have shown, and this is one of the most curious results of his investigations, that the same fungus does not incite or maintain the alcoholic, the acetic-acid, the lactic-acid, or the butyric-acid fermentations, but that these changes are produced by different species, nearly allied but distinguishable from one another under the microscope; the specific differences between them extending to this strange difference in their powers of nutrition or respiration, which induces different reactions in a fermentable fluid.* This may be said to have become perhaps the more prevailing opinion of the men of science of the day.

Baron Liebig, so recently lost to science and the world, was the great defender of the opposite view, that the division of sugar into alcohol and carbonic acid was a phenomenon belonging to a numerous class in chemistry, where compound bodies in a state of comparatively unstable equilibrium are resolved into simpler groups by taking on the motion of other bodies in contact with them and in the condition of motion, and experiencing the molecular movements attendant upon this particular kind of motion.

One of the most recent researches upon this subject is by Manassein, of St. Petersburg, under the direction of Dr. Wiesner, made in 1871. The result of his research is embodied in the following sentence: " *Upon the basis of all these experiments, I consider myself justified in maintaining that the living yeast-cell is not necessary to alcoholic fermentation.*" He adds, " *It is more than probable that the specific ferment in the living yeast-cell, and in some varieties of mold, is produced as the emulsion is in sweet almonds.*" It is well known that this emulsion produces fermentation without any instrumentality of organic forms.

182. Still more recent researches have shown that alcoholic fermentation attends the growth of several genera and numerous species of yeast-plants, from which it is plain that alcoholic fermentation is a phe-

---
perature be kept up, bubbles of carbonic-acid gas begin to rise from the fungus, which continues to grow, although more slowly. Fermentation sets in instead of putrefaction, and alcohol is produced in sensible quantities. The one great change which has been produced in the circumstances of the fungus is that it has now been almost wholly excluded from contact with free oxygen, while, in its former condition, it was bathed in it." Upon this change, according to Pasteur, depends its now acting as a ferment instead of inducing putrefaction.

* Nature, p. 80, 1872.—Address by Wyville Thompson.

nomenon attendant on a peculiar molecular condition which many microscopic plants pass through. Liebig always maintained that this was a dynamic condition, not necessarily connected with growth or vitality. This conclusion is supported by the startling discovery, made by Pasteur himself as well as by Lechartier and Bellamy, that sound fruits containing sugar, brought into an atmosphere free from oxygen, begin to produce carbonic acid and alcohol without the instrumentality of the fermentation of yeast. Pasteur held, in 1861, that oxygen is necessary to the growth of the yeast-plant. If the oxygen is present as such, or free, the plant consumes it, and partly assimilates the sugar and partly burns it. If the oxygen be not free, it is taken from the sugar. This view is not sustained by other and more recent researches.

183. O. Brefeld gives (in Wagner's *Repertorium*, 1873,) the following results of an investigation of the subject of alcoholic fermentation :

1. The alcohol-ferment requires, like all plants, for its development as a vegetable, the action of free oxygen.

2. In the exclusion of the air—the exclusion of free oxygen—the yeast-plant cannot grow.

3. It is a mistake to assume that the yeast-plant instead of free oxygen can take to its growth and increase combined oxygen from a body rich in this ingredient, like sugar, for example.

4. Again, it is a mistake that upon this accredited peculiarity of ferment to vegetate—to grow upon combined oxygen—the process of fermentation depends.

5. The alcoholic fermentation is excited by living yeast-cells that are shut off from free oxygen and do not grow.

6. The fermentation is in this case the expression of an abnormal, imperfect, vital process, in which the necessary material to the growth of the yeast-plant—the sugar, nitrogenous and mineral substances, and free oxygen—do not all work together to the simultaneous and harmonious growth of the yeast. The sugar by itself, or in mistaken relations to the other nutrient substances, will be decomposed and separated by the yeast-cells.

The yeast-cell which possesses the power in this abnormal vital process will show enfeebling of its vitality to continue for weeks.

7. The yeast-cell has great affinity for free oxygen; it possesses the power to grow in carbonic acid that contains less than $\frac{1}{6000}$ of its volume of free oxygen, and perfectly consume the whole of the oxygen. This affinity for free oxygen is not possessed by the lower types of mold, with the exception of *Mucor racemosus* and the nearest related organisms. The yeast-plant is, by reason of this property, an extremely fine reagent for oxygen.

8. By reason of the strong affinity of the yeast-plant for oxygen, united with its peculiarity of living in fluids, and rapidly to multiply and grow, there comes in fluid media, in which the yeast-plant grows, a *dearth of free oxygen*, and with it the phenomenon of fermentation, as, for example, in the art of beer-brewing.

9. There may arise in a fluid, fermentation and growth of the yeast-plant at the same time, even when the surface is in direct contact with the free air. Neither from a theoretical nor from a practical standpoint is the possibility shut out that fermentation and growth may both take place at the same instant in a yeast-cell; that, therefore, the growing yeast-cell which is in inharmonious relations to the free oxygen present may ferment the sugar it has absorbed.

184. EFFECTS OF FERMENTATION.—The action of the acids of ferment is well known. They tend to liquefy the gluten, and deprive it of its tenacity and elasticity. [With time, gluten dissolves in acetic acid; this being the foundation of one of the methods of determining the amount of gluten in the flour. The gluten is dissolved away from the starch; the starch weighed by itself; and the gluten determined, as we have seen, from the specific gravity of the solution.] It is also well known that dough too far advanced in fermentation (old leaven) yields offensive products both to the taste and smell, including butyric ether and other offensive products.

185. WHY HUNGARIAN FLOUR WILL MAKE LIGHT BREAD.—We are now able to see how the superiority of the Hungarian flour produced by the high-milling process is intimately connected with the production of the Vienna bread, which is entirely free from acidity and any offensive odor. The gluten encased in its cells, not having been crushed, is but slightly exposed to the action of the press-yeast. The press-yeast is capable of converting the starch into sugar, and sugar into alcohol and carbonic acid. The nitrogenous constituents, owing to their protection within cells, largely retain the integrity of their chemical constitution. The tendency to lactic fermentation, where portions of the gluten are in solution, and, as a consequence, of the acidity degrading or liquefying the gluten and so making the bread heavy and sour, or of butyric acid and other compounds, offensive to the taste and smell, would manifestly be increased by the rupture of the gluten-cells, which is produced in much larger measure in the process of low milling.

WHY BREAD MADE FROM OAT, RYE, OR BARLEY MEAL IS HEAVY.—We have hitherto spoken of gluten as the body upon the tenacity and elasticity of which the capacity of the moistened flour to hold gas-bubbles depends. Strictly speaking, this quality is due to a portion only of the body separated from the starch of flour by washing with water. The body so obtained, on treatment with alcohol, is resolved, as already pointed out, into two substances; one soluble and the other insoluble in alcohol. Of the portion soluble in alcohol, there are two, one called mucine—vegetable caseine, and the other called glutin, or glyadin, or vegetable gelatine. It is to this vegetable gelatine that the capacity to hold gas-bubbles is due, and it is because wheat contains a notable portion of it that this grain will yield a highly porous bread, and other cereal grains, oats, rye and barley, for example, which contain only traces of vegetable gelatine, yield only heavy bread or bread deficient in porosity. It is this vegetable gelatine, the degradation of which by acids produced in fermentation, and so causing a diminution of its tenacity, that deprives the walls of the cells in the sponge of their cohesion and allows it to collapse. It is in consequence of this liquefaction of the vegetable gelatine that flour which has from any cause become sour is no longer capable of making a light or highly cellular bread.

186. To counteract this deterioration, Liebig proposed the use of limewater, which arrests the liquefaction of the vegetable gelatine, and by some kind of combination restores more or less its tenacity. Ritthausen found that solution of sulphate of lime possessed the property of increasing the tenacity of gluten, and so facilitated its separation from the starch of flour by the process of washing. The same end is effected with inferior flours by the employment of small quantities of alum in solution in making the dough, and also in the use of small quantities of sulphate of copper and sulphate of zinc. All these agents have the effect of increasing the whiteness of the bread produced over that which would be produced by the simple process of fermentation. Mégé Mouriès conceives that the darkening of the dough, which sometimes occurs even in the use of white flour, is due to an excess of lactic fermentation produced by cerealine, the nitrogenous constituent soluble in water which he finds in the gluten-coat. This action which produces at first proportionally more dextrine, at a later period yields, at the expense of the gluten, ammonia and a brown substance. It is to the predominance of this ferment in the dough of black bread that its extreme dark color is to be ascribed. The presence of acetic and butyric or lactic acid is objectionable, because it tends to liquefy the gluten and make the bread heavy and sour to the taste; so also any offensive gases or ethers, such as accompany putrefactive fermentation; so also the degradation of color.

187. PROBLEM OF A BREAD YEAST.—It will be seen from the foregoing that the problem of a bread-yeast is the production of a yeast-plant capable, within a limited time, of producing *only* alcohol and carbonic acid; the alcohol by itself producing comparatively little effect upon the dough, and the carbonic acid serving only by its production of cellules or pores, in every part of the interior of the mass of dough, to give the bread lightness. Such a yeast was the ideal yeast sought by the Vienna bakers, and for which they offered their prize, won by Mautner, of St. Marks, Austria.

188. THE PRESS-YEAST.—Historically, the press-yeast dates back to 1847 and the introduction of the yeast from beer, only to 1817. Up to that time, the sour dough, and a mixture of sour dough and hops obtained by boiling, were the instrumentalities for producing porous bread throughout Austria and Southern Europe. At this time in Vienna there was introduced by the bakers a roll made with a finer quality of flour by the process of *sweet fermentation*, (that is, with yeast,) which was called the imperial roll, (*Kaiser-Semmel.*) From this time to 1840, nothing new appeared, though there was constant demand for the sweet fermented rolls.

PREPARATION OF YEAST.   87

At length, a prize was offered in 1845 by the Association of Vienna Bakers, (an association which has kept its records from the year 1452 down,) for the independent production of a good yeast, and the trades-union recognizing the importance of the object, offered to the discoverer the loan of its great gold medal. The offer of these prizes met with success in 1847. Adolf Ignaz Mautner, succeeded in producing the desired article, and in 1850 the prize and the medal were awarded for the production of his cereal press-yeast. From this point on, the baking-industry made rapid development throughout the Austrian empire, and at the Paris Exposition in 1867 the Vienna bakery was recognized as the first in the world. Vienna may therefore properly claim the double honor of having been the seat of the first development of the art of high milling and the birthplace of the use of press-yeast.

189. To give some idea of the development of this industry, the press yeast sold by A. I. Mautner & Son is herewith presented:

	Zollverein pounds
1846	72,400
1852	380,600
1862	1,144,500
1872	3,170,000

In recognition of the magnitude and importance of this branch of industry, the council of the international jury of 1873 gave to this firm the Grand diploma of Honor.

190. PREPARATION OF THE PRESS-YEAST.—The press-yeast is obtained by skimming the froth from the mash in active fermentation, which contains the upper yeast, and repeatedly washing it with cold water until only the pure white yeast settles clear from the water. This soft, tenacious mass, after the water has been drawn off, is gathered into bags and subjected to hydraulic pressure until there remains a semi-solid, somewhat brittle, dough-like substance, still containing 80 per cent. of water. This is the *press-yeast*. It is then resolved into packages of definite weight up to four pounds, and wrapped in paper, and supplied to the market. Such yeast in summer will keep for eight days, and for an indefinite time on ice.

191. There are several modes of producing the press-yeast. The writer visited the press-yeast manufactory of the Brothers Rheininghaus at Steinfeld, near Graz, Steyermark, which is upon a large scale, and the products of which attracted especial attention at the Exposition. In this establishment, both beer and alcohol are produced. In the preparation of the press-yeast, coarse rye-meal is preferred. The wheat-groats are less suited, probably because the excess of gluten interferes with the removal of the water by pressure. Potatoes can be employed, but the yeast produced is not so effective or lasting. Malt is employed to produce sugar. One part is enough for the perfect mashing of eighteen parts of flour. The mashing has for its office the conversion of starch into sugar. This takes place best at a temperature of 140° to 145° Fah-

renheit. In from two to six hours, the conversion into sugar is complete, which may be recognized by the sweet taste.

This solution is cooled to a temperature of from 75° to 80° Fahrenheit, and then active yeast should be added at the same temperature, stirred intimately, and left at a temperature of about 75°.

To facilitate the rising of the yeast-cells, an alkaline carbonate and diluted sulphuric acid are added. To every 100 pounds of the flour, half an ounce of oil of vitriol ($H O, S O_3$) diluted with water and its equivalent of bicarbonate of soda are employed.

The disengaged carbonic-acid gas in rising to the surface carries the yeast-cells up with it. The foam that rises to the surface is skimmed off and repeatedly washed with water. The water is drawn off from the yeast-cells that settle out at the bottom, and the white deposit gathered in cloth bags, and the excess of water removed by pressure.

192. Xavier Zettler, of Munich, employs a mixture of equal parts of rye-malt, unground wheat, and slowly roasted barley-malt. These three are intimately and finely ground together, and to this mixture 4 to 5 per cent. of steamed and dried finely-ground potatoes are added. These are made into a mash with water at a temperature of about 145° to 150° Fahrenheit; then sufficient water is added to make it into a uniform emulsion, which will carry the temperature down to 120°. To bring it back to the temperature for the production of sugar, (from 140° to 150°,) water of a temperature of 200° is added with constant stirring. The mash remains now from twenty to twenty-four hours, during which the lactic acid produced liquefies the gluten. When this has taken place, which prepares the mash for rapid fermentation, the emulsion is rapidly cooled by the addition of cold water and the employment of a cooling-apparatus to the temperature of 75° to 80°, and the yeast added in the proportion of four parts yeast to a hundred of the malt-mixture. This mixture is stirred up in fresh water, and added to a small quantity of the mash in a separate vessel, in which the fermentation proceeds rapidly. When it has attained its highest activity, it will be returned to the whole mass. This now remains ten to twelve hours, during which the perfect fermentation will have commenced, and the whole mass have gone over to the period of the production of yeast-cells. When this period has closed, which will be indicated by the falling of the mash, the foam will be skimmed off, repeatedly mashed in fresh water, permitted to settle out, collected, and pressed.

The details of the processes pursued in the establishment of Rheininghans, at Steinfeld, and of Mautner & Son, in St. Marks, I am not in position to communicate.

Before proceeding to the description of the use of the press-yeast, it may be well to glance at the other processes of making bread in use in Germany and France, which have gained a place among the bakers of those countries.

193. The PUMPERNICKEL OF WESTPHALIA, which is made from whole

rye-meal, and which is substantially the black bread produced by slow baking in large loaves, and used among the lower classes, and in the armies of Eastern Europe, is *usually* made without the use of yeast, employing only the leaven or dough of the previous batch to secure the desired porosity.

The ordinary bread of rye-flour, or of mixed wheat and rye, made in loaves, and so extensively in use in Germany and Austria among the peasant classes, and also among the higher classes, because of its greater nutritive value than the bread made from the higher grades of wheat-flour, is now generally made with the aid of yeast.

194. PARIS WHEAT-BREAD.—In Paris, the wheat-bread is produced in the following manner: The fermentation is made to depend chiefly upon the gluten of the dough; yeast being employed merely to introduce and facilitate the action.

1. A lump of dough remaining from the last batch of bread, consisting of 8 pounds of flour and 4 pounds of water, 12 pounds, is set aside at eight o'clock in the evening. This is left till the next morning at six o'clock, and constitutes the so-called fresh leaven.

2. This is then kneaded with 8 pounds of meal and 4 pounds of water, which gives the once revived leaven, 12 pounds.

3. At two o'clock in the afternoon, the baker kneads in 16 pounds of flour and 8 pounds of water, and this gives the second revived leaven, 24 pounds.

4. At five o'clock in the afternoon, he adds 100 pounds of flour and 52 pounds of water, to which from two to three tenths of a pound of yeast have been added, making 152.2 pounds, and altogether, of dough, 200 pounds.

5. At seven o'clock in the evening, he adds to this dough 132 pounds of flour and 68 pounds of water, with from three to six tenths of a pound of yeast and 2 pounds of salt, and kneads the whole to a mass of dough, which weighs altogether about 402 pounds.

From this portion of dough, he makes five batches of bread in the following way:

First baking: He takes half of the dough, fashions it into loaves of the proper size and form, sets it aside for a while at a temperature of 70° Fahrenheit to rise, and then puts it in the oven to bake. The bread so obtained has a sour taste and dark color.

Second baking: The half of the remaining dough is mixed with 132 pounds of flour and about 68 pounds of water, from three to six tenths of a pound of yeast and 2 pounds of salt, and the whole immediately kneaded. Half of this product is taken for the second baking. It is whiter and better than the first baking.

Third baking: The remaining half of the dough left from the second baking is mixed with 132 pounds of flour and 68 pounds of water, containing three-tenths of a pound of yeast and two pounds of salt, and the whole immediately kneaded. The third baking is made from the half of the so prepared dough.

The fourth baking is prepared like the third.

Fifth baking: This is prepared as the preceding, and yields fancy bread, the finest quality produced.

195. MÉGÉ MOURIÈS'S METHOD.—Mégé Mouriès has sought to introduce an improved method of bread-making. It is bread resting upon a mode of grading the products of milling, so as to yield from 100 pounds of wheat—

72.72 pounds of flour and white groats;
15.72 pounds of brown groats;
11.56 pounds of bran.

At six o'clock in the evening, to 40 pounds of water, at a temperature of 70°, he adds the tenth of a pound of grape-sugar, and seven hundredths of a pound of yeast. This mixture he leaves over night at a temperature of 70°. At six o'clock the next morning, the fluid will be saturated with carbonic acid. He then stirs in the brown groats, 15.72 pounds, when the fermentation immediately begins. At two o'clock, he adds 30 pounds of water, and passes the mixture through a hair-sieve to separate the bran from the added groats. The mixture separated from the bran weighs about 55 pounds. To this he adds the 72.72 pounds of flour, and seven-tenths of a pound of salt, and kneads the whole to a dough. The dough will be fashioned into loaves, in which the fermentation will go on, and then placed in the oven to be baked.

196. By this process, Mégé Mouriès uses the 72.72 pounds of white flour and about 12.72 pounds which come from the brown groats. This process, although promising a larger percentage of white bread from a given weight of wheat, does not seem to have met with extensive introduction.

197. The method accredited to the London bakers is the following: The process contemplates the consumption of a sack of flour weighing 280 pounds. For this flour, 5 or 6 pounds of boiled potatoes freed from their skins, rubbed with from 2 to 3 pounds of the flour and one quart of fluid beer-yeast, and then intimately stirred with sufficient water to make the whole a uniform thin emulsion. Fermentation commences almost immediately, and after three hours the ferment may be used. It is at its maximum in about four or five hours. To this, 20 pounds of water are added, and the flour worked in till a stiff dough is formed. This is set in a warm place to ferment. At the end of an hour, the *bubbles* begin to swell the mass, soon the carbonic-acid gas escapes, and the dough falls. Soon after a second accumulation of gas-bubbles takes place and escapes.

The next operation consists in diffusing this dough in water, making about 150 pounds in all, adding to this uniform emulsion 2 to 4 pounds of salt, according to taste, and then working in the balance of the meal.

The dough is allowed to stand for $1\frac{1}{2}$ or 2 hours, and then fashioned into $4\frac{1}{4}$-pound loaves, which are put into an oven of about 572° Fahrenheit at the beginning, which falls to from 400° to 430° in the hour of baking. This process yields 94 so-called 4-pound loaves.

These two methods are circumstantial to the last degree. The Vienna method, which rests upon the use of *press*-yeast, as will be seen, is much simpler.

198. SUBSTITUTES FOR FERMENT.—The discovery that the essential thing to making bread porous was a spring of carbonic-acid gas in every part of the moistened flour was made elsewhere as well as in Germany. Fifty years ago, in this country, bread was made by employing, in the place of leaven, sour milk and bicarbonate of potash, (saleratus.) The acid of sour milk (lactic acid) united with the potassa of the carbonate, and, setting the carbonic acid free, gave porosity to the dough. Thirty years ago, cream tartar (the acid tartrate of potassa) was substituted for the sour milk, and bicarbonate of soda for bicarbonate of potassa. The cream tartar had the advantage over sour milk that, being a powder, it could be weighed, and thus the proper proportion be taken to exactly neutralize the soda of the bicarbonate, also a powder, and invariably yield a white biscuit or bread. Besides this, the sour milk, varying in the proportion of its lactic acid, would, from its imperfectly neutralizing the soda, sometimes leave a portion of that constituent to discolor the product.

As a substitute for sour milk, diluted hydrochloric acid was employed in England, in the bread, with bicarbonate of soda, yielding common salt, which is a necessary constituent of farinaceous food. The attempt was made to saturate the dry flour with hydrochloric acid, so that the flour so prepared could, when required for use, be intimately mixed by sifting with another portion of flour, with which an equivalent of bicarbonate of soda had been intimately mixed, and then the whole stirred up with water and immediately baked.

Baron Liebig modified this process, adapting it to the whole meal of rye or wheat, with a view to the increase of the nutritive value, by preventing the loss consequent upon fermentation of the dark bread in use among the lower classes in Germany.

199. In England, tartaric acid, obtained from cream tartar, was mingled with its equivalent of bicarbonate of soda, and this mixture with flour, yielding what was called a *self-raising flour*. It required only the addition of milk or water, in proper proportion to make a dough, and this might be immediately introduced into the oven and baked. The tartaric acid and bicarbonate of soda promptly dissolving and reacting on each other in the water or milk, disengaged the carbonic acid, giving porosity to the dough, and with the baking the desired cellular structure of the bread.

200. DAUGLISH'S METHOD, AERATED BREAD.—The method of making bread, invented and introduced into England by Dr. Dauglish, recognized that the essential quality of an agent for making the dough porous was a spring of carbonic acid in every part of the moistened flour, and carried out to practical working, the idea of mixing the flour in a confined space with water charged under pressure with carbonic acid, (soda-water.) The dough so formed, on coming to the

air of ordinary atmospheric pressure, expanded under the influence of the expanding carbonic acid until the whole possessed the cellular structure of thoroughly leavened dough, when it was immediately put into the oven and baked.

These various processes, like the yeast and leaven processes, contemplated no addition to the nutritive value of the bread.

201. PHOSPHATIC BREAD.—A process having in view increased nutritive value to the bread, which was exhibited at the Vienna Exhibition at the request of the Archduke Albert and the minister of war of the Austrian government, will be described in the appendix, under the head of phosphatic bread.

202. CHANGES OF FLOUR IN BECOMING BREAD.—In popular use, we employ the word "bread" to qualify loaves which are served in slices. The rolls are much smaller. Both consist alike of crumb and crust. The crumb is made up of a multitude of cells of thin walls containing carbonic-acid gas, the product of fermentation in the dough. These walls of the cells contain both gluten and starch and traces of dextrine and sugar. As a consequence of the treatment of water and the application of heat, the starch-grains, which, in their normal condition, are little sacs filled with minute granules of starch proper, have been swollen and burst. Starch similarly treated by itself, as in the preparation for stiffening linen in the laundry, when dried in a thin layer upon glass plate, for example, is transparent and presents a glazed surface. When this glazed material is removed with a knife-blade, it is seen to be stiff and horny. The gluten, which is mixed with it in the crumb of bread, and which may be conceived to be continuous, however thin throughout the wall of the cell, has been, by the process of baking, dehydrated; that is, the heat to which it has been subjected has driven out a certain amount of water, which chemically sustains something like the same relation to the gluten from which it has been expelled that the water expelled by heat from alum-crystals sustains to the original body of alum. This is the condition of the gluten from the crumb in the interior of the loaf at the instant of its removal from the oven. On drying, it abstracts the water from the starch with which it is coated, or intimately mixed, as the roasted alum absorbs the water that is sprinkled upon it. The starch by this process being dried and stiffened, gives its support to the walls of the cell, and renders the texture of the stale loaf more firm than that of the fresh loaf.

203. That the starch has undergone no especial change as the result of fermentation, beyond its conversion into glacial starch and the conversion of a certain small amount into dextrine or gum-sugar (glucose) and alcohol and carbonic-acid gas, is evident from the reaction which it gives with solution of iodine.

It has taken on a property, which we observe in the boiled starch of the laundry, of drying in thin layers to a transparent, horn-like varnish, less readily taken up by water.

The starch has also, in the mixing and kneading of the dough, become

PROCESS OF CHANGING FLOUR TO BREAD. 93

incorporated with the gluten, so that after baking, when it has become the glassy starch, it is no longer possible to separate the gluten as a distinct elastic body, such as may be produced from flour.

The gluten has been to some extent consumed in the process of fermentation, more especially in that form of it discussed by Mégé Mouriès, where the bread is dark and sweet, and in which I have observed the presence of ammonia. In the alcoholic fermentation, the degradation of the gluten is less.

204. The examination of the crust shows that heat has produced a variety of effects of marked character. The application of the iodine test shows that the starch is no longer present. It has been converted into dextrine.* Portions of the dextrine, as well as of the gluten, have been subjected to slight destructive distillation, yielding at the outset, with proper temperature, an agreeable essential oil, the grateful aroma of warm, freshly-baked rolls. If continued too long, the destructive distillation produced causes the formation of substances less grateful to the sense of smell, bitter to the taste, and worthless for purposes of nutrition. Among the bodies thus produced, Reichenbach recognizes *assamar*, a bitter substance, the effects of which on the human organism, according to v. Bibra, are akin to those of coffee.

205. In large loaves of bread, the thickness of the unpalatable crust is sometimes nearly half an inch, and this is not unfrequently sacrificed where such bread is made for the use of armies in the field.

206. Another effect of baking, and which is one of the chief results, is the coagulation of the vegetable albumen, one of the nitrogenous constituents of the flour, which is soluble in water, and which, diffused over the walls of the cells, contributes to their rigidity, and unites with the tenacious vegetable gelatine and the glassy starch in preventing the cell-walls from easily giving way after the requisite temperature has been maintained a sufficient length of time.

207. The test for phosphoric acid in the crumb, ammonio-sulphate of copper, or, better, ammonio-nitrate of silver, will show that the phosphatic constituents of the flour, as a part of the nitrogenous constituents, are present in every part of all the cells of well-made bread, and, therefore, that portions of the albuminoid bodies have been dissolved in the water used in making the dough.

* The baker is well aware of the presence of gum, or dextrine, in the crust. If, by chance, the just baked loaf, instead of being removed from the bake-pan, is allowed to remain in it, the vapor of water, escaping from the fresh loaf as a consequence of the elevated temperature, striking the tin, which has cooled from exposure to the air outside of the oven, is condensed to water between the tin and the loaf, and, dissolving the dextrine in the crust, makes the surface of the loaf below the margin of the bake-pan moist and sticky.

It is well known that thin slices of toast may be digested in a sensitive stomach without producing the distress occasioned by flatulency, and which, when fresh warm yeast-bread is eaten, is due to fermentation. The process of toasting has not only destroyed the yeast-germs, but it has converted the starch into dextrine, which is incapable of fermentation, and so of course incapable of producing flatulency.

208. The principal desirable effect of the heat in baking the bread, as we have seen, is, therefore, the coagulation of the albumen in the cell-walls, by which their permanency has largely been secured, to the advantage of the office of digestion and the destruction of the yeast-plant, as the cellular structure provides for the imbibition of the digestive fluids. The change wrought in the gluten is seen in the impossibility of obtaining it by any process of kneading and washing applied to the crumb of the loaf. We now see why it is necessary that the heat applied to the exterior of the loaf should be longer continued where the mass is large than where it is small; why small rolls may be baked in from ten to fifteen minutes with a temperature of 500° to 550° Fahrenheit, while a large loaf may require from one to three hours, according to the size. As the heat must be continued until the required change in the vegetable albumen has extended to the heart of the loaf, and as this takes time in proportion to the diameter of the loaf, we see why the surface may be burned before the interior is properly cooked; and, as a corollary, we see that the smaller the loaf the less change the surface will experience, the less injury it will receive during the time of its necessary stay in the oven to complete the cooking of the interior.

209. To prevent the burning of the crust, and yet produce loaves of considerable size, ovens are in use in Austria, and to some extent in this country, in which, until the mass of dough is thoroughly cooked, the loaf is surrounded by steam; this also prevents the too rapid formation of crust, and its subsequent cracking, consequent upon the increasing pressure of the heated gases of the interior, and so preserves a smooth exterior to the loaf.

210. The Austrian bakery in the Paris Exposition in 1867, for the production of loaf-bread, was provided with the steam-arrangement; but the oven of the Vienna bakery, on exhibition at the Vienna Exposition for the production of rolls, was a dry oven. One of the effects of heat in baking is that of destroying the yeast-plant, as already mentioned; this, however, is incomplete, as has been shown by Dr. Wiesner. To a certain extent, therefore, the yeast-plants continue to live for some time after the bread has been baked. It is partly to avoid the introduction of these living organisms that the universal practice prevails in Europe of eating the bread cold or stale. Another advantage is also gained by allowing the bread to become cold and dry. It is that the cell-walls coated with glassy starch—which renders them moist and adhesive when the bread is fresh and warm, and so disposes the bread to ball and become less pervious to the digestive fluids*—lose this adhesiveness on cooling by the absorption of the water from the glassy starch by the

---

* It is obvious that if the yeast-bread be eaten while warm, in the process of mastication it will become resolved by pressure into compact boluses, (the moist glassy starch being adhesive,) which having lost their cellular texture will resist the penetration of the gastric juices. Experiments made by Dr. Hammond, late Surgeon-General of the United States, who pressed the recently-baked yeast-bread into compact condition, showed that they resisted much longer the digestive powers of the stomach.

gluten in contact with it in the cell-walls; which water of hydration, as will be more clearly seeen, had been driven from the gluten to the starch by the elevated temperature of baking.

211. WHAT IS STALE BREAD ?—Experiments made by the writer to determine the cause of the moistening of the interior of dry stale bread by the process of toasting furnished the material for the explanation.

Boussingault many years ago undertook the solution of this problem. He first showed that, in becoming stale, bread did not necessarily lose weight, as of water. He cooled recently-baked bread in hermetically-sealed spaces, and it became stale. He then sealed stale bread in a metallic tube and heated it. It became fresh, and again became stale on cooling. He repeated the process again and again, in all, forty times with the same sample, alternately heating and cooling, and with the last heating it became fresh, and with the last cooling it became stale. He concluded from his experiments that there was what he called a *molecular* change in the crumb when heating, and again when cooling, and he thought he had explained it. Thenard, who listened to Boussingault's paper before the Academy, suggested that bread was a hydrate, from which water was driven out by heat and re-absorbed by cooling; but it would seem that according to this view fresh bread should be the drier of the two. Neither explanation was satisfactory. When I found that gluten was a hydrate from which a moderate heat would expel water, and that, on cooling, this water was again taken into the constitution of the gluten, I applied this fact to the solution of the problem. The stale crumb may be regarded as a frame-work of gluten, coated with glassy, dried starch, which is not readily dissolved by saliva. Of course, when taken into the mouth, it requires time before it becomes flexible, so as to be easily compressed and force out the fluids it takes up by virtue of its capillary action. But by heating, the water of hydration of the gluten is driven out; the starch which invests the gluten is moistened and rendered flexible; and the whole crumb, recovering the sponge-like elasticity of fresh bread, yields its juices when masticated, and is palatable. To test this, I placed in one end of a glass tube a quantity of thoroughly air-dried gluten, and hermetically sealed it; I then placed the end containing the gluten in warm water, and beheld a few moments later moisture condensing on the interior of the upper portion of the tube, which was cool. On withdrawing the tube from the water after a few hours, the film of moisture had disappeared. Water had been driven out from the gluten by heat, and had been re-absorbed on cooling. I then placed another quantity of gluten in the bottom of a tube, above it a tuft of cotton, and above the cotton a quantity of loose shavings of very thin glacial starch. Now I expected that if moisture was given off from the gluten, it would penetrate to the space occupied by the shavings, half liquefy the glacial starch, and make it adhesive. In this condition, the starch-shavings would be gummed fast to the glass, and it would no longer be possible to shake them about.

212. The experiment realized my expectations. The solution then of the question of the difference between stale bread and bread freshened by heating or by toasting is this: *The gluten of the crumb-walls of stale bread which are stiff and brittle is dehydrated by the heat in freshening, and the water of hydration driven out softens the glacial, horny starch which coats and penetrates the gluten. Thus softened, the crumb is more palatable, because it is in condition to be dissolved by the saliva, and tasted. On cooling, the water is withdrawn from the starch, which is thereby rendered stiff, and restored to the gluten, and the bread becomes stale.*

213. EFFECTS OF HEAT IN BAKING.—The effect of the heat in baking, as shown in the difference between the composition of the crumb and crust of wheaten roll free from water:

	Crumb.	Crust.
Nitrogenous ingredients	11.296	10.967
Dextrine, gum, and soluble starch	14.975	16.092
Sugar	4.175	4.149
Oil	1.683	0.715
Starch	67.871	68.077

214. The crust has lost about one-half its oil, and a little of its nitrogen and sugar. It has gained in dextrine and soluble starch. The crumb has lost in starch, perhaps in the process of fermentation, which would be sooner checked in the crust.

The relative amounts of water in the crumb and crust and total loaf of bread, as determined by Professor v. Fehling, are:

	Per cent.
For the total loaf	44.30
For the crumb	48.92
For the crust	16.23

A peculiarity of bread made from the use of yeast or leaven, where the kneading has been prolonged, and which is conceived to be an evidence of its superior excellence, is the so-called "*pile.*"

215. WHAT IS PILE?—This term, familiar to bakers, indicates, when prefaced by the epithet "good," and applied to bread, that a loaf so distinguished may be separated into strips, somewhat like the husks that coat an ear of Indian corn, or the coats that invest an onion. How this should appear in a loaf produced from a body apparently so homogeneous as dough is thought quite extraordinary. The explanation is, however, quite simple. Where the gluten of the flour is unimpaired by heat or souring, it retains its tenacity, even when greatly attenuated. When the dough is kneaded, it is spread out and folded over upon itself, again and again, from the border to the center; the surface is repeatedly dusted with flour, until these thin layers of flour, at last after long-continued kneading are everywhere present in the loaf, separating thin sheets and strips of fermented dough, each strip containing fibers of tenacious gluten. Now this fine flour constitutes a series of films of relatively diminished cohesion, so that when the loaf

is baked there are planes of easy separation alternating with sheets of tenacious crumb, having a direction from the bottom around the outside toward the center of the top, corresponding with the last foldings of the mass of dough, before placing it in the pan. These permit the loaf to be stripped off in coats, somewhat as pie-crust may be separated into flakes, and for a kindred reason. The pie-crust has been made by alternating layers of dough with layers of butter, and repeated foldings, to be followed with alternating extensions under the roller.

216. WHAT IS THE LOSS IN NUTRITIVE VALUE DUE TO THE PROCESS OF FERMENTATION?—This loss has been estimated by Dauglish as high as 10 per cent. It is due to the growth of the yeast-plant at the expense of the nitrogenous constituents of the flour, and to the conversion of starch into dextrine and sugar, and subsequently into alcohol and carbonic acid, both of which are lost; but which, in the conversion into gas and expansion by the heat of baking, give the raised loaf, which is about nine-tenths pores, or air-spaces, and one-tenth bread-substance. This estimated loss is conceived to be much too high. Heeren found the actual loss in weight to be 1.46 per cent., estimated on the anhydrous substance. Von Bibra found it but 2.1 per cent. Normandy's calculation, based on the production of carbonic acid to produce porosity, gives it at 2 per cent. The error in the high estimate is to be ascribed to the greater quantity of water which the unfermented porous bread is capable of holding.

217. THE QUESTION OF SIZE OF LOAF.—The Vienna bakers recognize in its fullest significance the proper relations between the crust and the crumb; so fixing the size of the mass of dough and so fixing the temperature of the oven that the bread when taken from the oven shall, every part of it, crust and crumb, be thoroughly cooked, none of it burned, and the whole, when warm, have an agreeable aroma, and, when cold, but fresh, shall be palatable in the highest degree without the addition of butter or edibles of any kind whatsoever.

7 V B

CHAPTER IV.

PROCESSES IN THE VIENNA BAKERY.

218. THE PREPARATION OF THE DOUGH FOR THE PRODUCTION OF VIENNA WHITE BREAD, THE IMPERIAL ROLL.—In nothing was the exposition of the Association of Vienna Bakers more striking than in its simplicity and cleanliness. Three classes of products were continuously turned out: first, the imperial roll, (the Vienna bread *par excellence ;*) secondly, the loaf of rye and wheat bread and the loaf of pure rye-bread ; thirdly, fancy bread, fruited cakes, sweet cakes, &c.

In the latter division, the variety produced was immense. With regard to both these and the forms of rye and rye and wheat loaves, it is not purposed to go into farther detail.

Fig. 70.

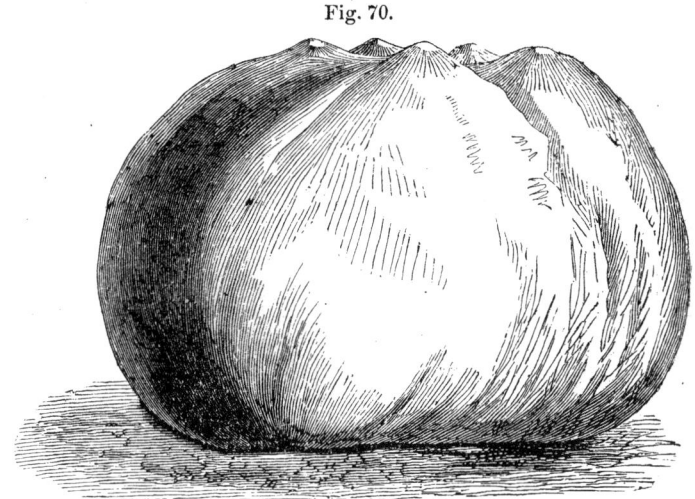

Kaiser-Semmel, or Imperial table-roll of Vienna.

219. IMPERIAL ROLL, (or *Kaiser-Semmel.*)—The bakery connected with the production of these rolls consisted of three departments : first, a store-room containing salt, fresh milk for daily consumption, and flour ; secondly, the dough-room ; and, thirdly the oven-room ; in the store-room, the sacks of fine flour, including the best 45 per cent. of the high-milled best Hungarian wheat, or a smaller percentage if the wheat was not of the best quality, embracing the grades from the imperial extra to No. 5.

For the best imperial rolls made at the Vienna bakery, they employed

DOUGH FOR VIENNA BREAD.

only the first four grades, Nos. 0, 1, 2, and 3, about 18 to 25 per cent. of the total wheat. These grades were also employed for the production of the tea-cakes, containing milk and butter, the *Gipfel*, or pinnacle cake, which has the form of a crescent, and contains milk and lard, and the *Brioche*, an oblong, slender roll, containing milk and sugar, neither of them containing water, mixed with the milk

220. The dough-room was an oblong apartment, well lighted on two sides. Along the center were racks for the support of long, smoothly-planed, movable boards, on which the dough-balls of the *Kaiser-Semmel* were placed for transportation to the oven. Along one whole side, and a part of two others, was a broad shelf, or continuous table, breast-high, for handling the dough. Opposite the long table was a sink, and a supply of hot and cold water. At one end was a zinc-lined trough, about two feet and a half wide and about eight feet long, semicylindrical in form, for setting the sponge and—

221. PREPARING THE DOUGH. Into the middle of this trough, flour was emptied from the sacks, leaving the ridge sloping down to the ends. Into a pail holding about five gallons, equal parts of milk and water were poured and left to stand until the mixture acquired the temperature of the room, which was between 70° and 80° Fahrenheit. It is then poured into one end of the trough, and intimately mixed, with the aid of the naked hands and arms, with a small amount of flour, making a thin emulsion. To this three and one-half ounces of press-yeast by weight, after finely crumbling in the hands, to every three quarts of the liquid, and one ounce of fine salt, were added, and intimately diffused throughout the mixture. The trough was then covered and left undisturbed for three-quarters of an hour. At the end of this time, the workmen, step by step, thoroughly incorporated from the neighboring pile an amount of flour sufficient to give the requisite texture to the dough. The determination of this point belongs to the department of unwritten art, but practically does not probably vary in first quality of flour, day by day, five ounces in fifty pounds from the proportion indicated in the following table given me by Roman Uhl:

    8 pounds of flour;
    3 quarts of mixed milk and water in equal proportions;
    3½ ounces of press-yeast;
    1 ounce of salt.

The mass of dough so prepared is covered and left for two hours and a half, at the end of which time it presents a smooth, tenacious, puffed, homogeneous mass of slightly yellowish color, which, when subjected to the pressure of the hand, yields to indentation without rupture, and on withdrawing the hand recovers, in a short time, but not instantly, its original outline and smooth surface. It is now in condition to be weighed into pound masses, and cut with a convenient machine into twelve smaller masses of uniform equal weight, and having a thickness of about three-quarters of an inch. Workmen take individually these smaller flat masses, lay the back of the forefinger of one hand upon each one in turn, and with the thumb and forefinger of the other hand draw out slightly each corner of the irregular mass, and fold it over to the center, to be secured by pressure and adhesion, when the whole is reversed, and placed upon the smooth board, already mentioned, to complete the fermentation preparatory to being transferred to the oven. Before being introduced into the oven, the little rolls are again reversed, and restored to their original position, having considerably increased in volume, to be still farther enlarged in the oven to at least twice the volume of the original dough. They were distributed over the bottom of the oven near to, but not touching, each other, where they remained for about fifteen minutes, when they were taken out, with the same long-handled, thin, flat, wooden shovel, or spatula, on which they were introduced. As all parts of the oven are not alike heated, some of the rolls are likely to bake more rapidly than others, and the workman who opens the door to examine them from time to time changes their places, replacing the more exposed with others from a less heated portion of the oven, so that but a small proportion are rejected as culls from having been overbaked. If it is desired to glaze the surface, they are touched in the process of baking with a sponge dipped in milk, which, besides imparting to them a smooth surface, increases the brilliancy of the slightly reddish cinnamon-color, and adds to the grateful aroma of the crust.

222. THE OVEN.—In regard to the construction of the Vienna oven, there seems to be nothing of complexity to challenge attention. It was made of brick, presenting the edges and not the flat surfaces, having a very low arch. The floor was oblong-oval in form, having an inclination toward the door of about eight degrees. The ovens in the city were built substantially on the same simple plan.

The oven was fired eight times in the twenty-four hours with dry ight wood. The baking for the day commenced at two o'clock in the morning and closed late in the afternoon. The person in charge of the oven of the Exposition was introducing and withdrawing the rolls and changing their place from cooler to warmer places or the reverse at short intervals during the whole time between two firings. As the rolls were brought out, any that were overbrowned were culled out, to be sold elsewhere than at the Exposition restaurant, and at a cheaper rate.

223. Fig. 71 is a vertical section through the greatest depth, and Fig. 72 a section through the greatest horizontal diameter, of the average *Kaiser-Semmel*, of which 12 weigh 500 grams, one-half a kilogram. One *Kaiser-Semmel* weighs 643 Troy grains.

224. ADVANTAGES OF THE VIENNA BREAD—SECRET OF ITS EXCELLENCE.—From what has been said, it will be apparent that the virtues of this bread had their origin primarily in the Hungarian wheat. These are not due to any particular variety of wheat, or to any marked peculiarity of soil or mode of fertilizing, or to a mean annual temperature

CAUSES OF SUPERIORITY. 101

characterizing the climate of Hungary as a whole, but, as already intimated, to a *peculiarity of the climate*, uniting special dryness of the air during the hot season, from the time of the development of the milk of the berry through the period of its segregation of the various constituents of the grain, down to its being housed for thrashing.

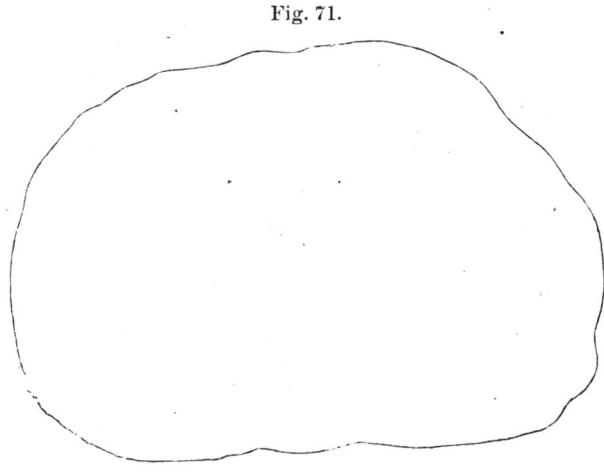

Fig. 71.

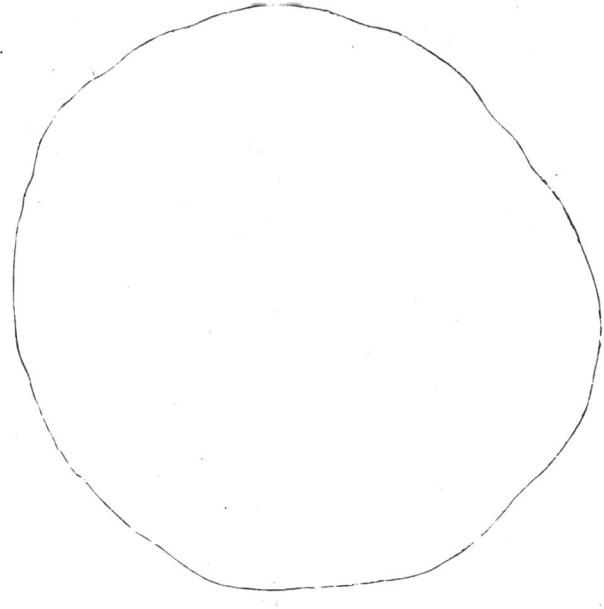

Fig. 72.

With a view to finding out what influence the climate of Hungary exerts on wheat, I have been furnished by Graf Zichy with several samples of great interest. They are original Australian white wheat, and the produce of a portion of the same sample, on Hungarian soil, after some years. The changes, if one might form a conclusion from so limited a range of observation, seem to be, in the first place, (*a*) from white more or less to redness, that is, a change in the amount of red or orange pigment in the color or seed coat; and (*b*) a change to a more flinty quality of the grain; and (*c*) a more shrunken berry; in the second place, to the process of grits or high milling, by which the *organized forms* of the grain are *disintegrated* or detached from each other *without crushing*, and *opening* the gluten-cells, which renders the flour produced by the low-milling process liable to become musty and sour; in the third place, to the employment of a selected portion of the flour so produced, varying, according to the quality of the wheat ground, from 25 to 45 per cent. of the whole grain; and, in the fourth place, to the introduction of press-yeast, which renders the process of making dough *quantitative*, and less a work of art; avoids the lactic, acetic, and other offensive fermentations; and yields a bread, the dough of which has been subjected to the process of purely vinous fermentation, producing only alcohol and carbonic acid, and imparting no taste due to the action of yeast; and, lastly, to the production of the bread in rolls or loaves, so small as to provide for the thorough cooking of the interior, at the same time that a thin, aromatic, palatable crust of substantially unimpaired nutritive qualities has been uniformly produced over all the surface, without any portion of it having been rendered inedible from heat too high or too prolonged. The temperature of the oven at the Vienna Exposition was not far from 500° Fahrenheit.

225. As the coagulation of the albumen, which is the principal change that takes place in the cooking of the loaf, is affected at a temperature below 212° Fahrenheit, and as flour is not browned except at a temperature much above this point, it is easy to see how skillfully the Vienna baker has adapted the size of the roll to the object to be gained. Where the loaves are large, the surface must be protected by baking at a prolonged lower temperature, or by surrounding the loaves with steam until nearly the close of the process of baking, which prevents the formation of the inedible crust. With the latter arrangement, wheat and rye loaves of a pound weight were shown the jury at the steam-bakeries at Wittingau, one of the seats of Prince Schwarzenberg, which loaves were encased in a thin crust of exceeding delicacy and palatableness, and presented a crumb of uniform lightness and most acceptable taste.

226. ADVANTAGE TO THE CONSUMER OF ROLLS RATHER THAN LOAVES.—The mode of producing bread in Vienna, where all the baking is in public bakeries, enables the householder to place upon his table day by day absolutely fresh bread in precisely the quantity required for consumption. He thereby escapes the waste attendant upon the accumulation of stale bread, and he also avoids the deterioration and

losses attendant upon keeping a stock of flour in his house. He may thus have a better bread with the expenditure of a given sum of money than he could have if he maintained all the appointments of a bakery within his own dwelling.

227. CAN WE HAVE VIENNA BREAD IN AMERICA?—The answer in general is, we may. To assure it, we must have, first, as good flour as the bakers of Vienna have; second, we must use the press-yeast; and, third, we must pursue the same processes of preparing the dough and baking.

Good flour can only be made from sound, pure wheat, and, having the wheat to start with, by good milling; and this means, in general, flinty wheat reduced by the process of high or half-high milling, and a selection of the products of the milling, not to exceed one-half of the total weight of the wheat ground. Good, fresh middlings flour would compare favorably with the average Hungarian flour.

Press-yeast is now produced in this country. It should be of recent preparation; sweet, so that it will yield only alcohol and carbonic acid as products of fermentation.

228. The sponge should be made with a mixture of half milk and half water. The proportions of the ingredients, temperature, and the processes of preparation of the dough in bulk and detail as given in the account of Vienna bread in the 221st paragraph, will give the unbaked loaf.

In general these proportions are:
  8 pounds of flour;
  3 quarts of mixed water and milk in equal proportions;
  3½ ounces of press-yeast;
  1 ounce of salt.

229. The baking requires an oven of no especial complexity, but should be capable of maintaining a constant temperature of about 500° Fahrenheit.

The loaves should be of size to require not more than from 15 to 20 minutes to bake completely; that is, to thoroughly cook the interior by the time the outside has assumed a delicate thin reddish or cinnamon-brown crust, and become palatable in every part. If eaten at its best, that is, soon after it has cooled, or at least during the day of its preparation, it will not fall behind the average first quality of Vienna *Kaiser-Semmel*.

APPENDIX A.

230. DEMPWOLFF'S INVESTIGATION OF THE HUNGARIAN WHEAT AND WHEAT-FLOUR FURNISHED FROM THE PESTH WALZMÜHLE, (CYLINDER-MILL.)—The flour in this year (1869) was 78 per cent. of the wheat; the bran, 22 per cent. These were included in fourteen distinct products. The flour was produced from a mixture of two-thirds Theis and one-third Banat wheat, of which the analysis of the whole grain gave—

Water	10.51
Ash	1.50
Nitrogen	2.24
Starch	65.41

The ash of the whole grain yielded in 100 parts—

Fe_2O_3	0.404
CaO	4.275
MgO	14.862
KO	31.825
NaO	1.016
PO_5	49.912
SO_3	0.101
CO_2	0.086
	102.481

The ash contained—

Water	10.5	Lime	4.275
Ash	1.5	Magnesia	14.862
Gluten	14.4	Potash	31.825
Starch	65.4	Soda	1.016
Oil and woody fiber	8.2	Phosphoric acid	49.902

231. The products of the milling gave in 100 parts—

A and B, 0.489 grits.

No. 0, 3.144 ⎫
No. 1, 2.635 ⎪
No. 2, 5.291 ⎬ imperial extra flour.
No. 3, 7.165 ⎭

No. 4, 14.757 ⎫
No. 5, 17.935 ⎬ roll-flour.

No. 6, 15.419 ⎫
No. 7, 6.805 ⎬ bread-flour.

No. 8, 2.576 black flour.

No. 9, 9.516 ⎫
No. 10, 9.000 ⎬ bran.

No. 11, 1.290 clippings.

3.988 loss.

HUNGARIAN WHEAT AND FLOUR.

232. From this wheat, 100 parts yielded—

Groats and extra imperial flour	18.724
Semmel or roll flour, Nos. 4 and 5	32.682
Bread-flour, Nos. 6 and 7	22.224
Black flour, No. 8	2.576
Bran	18.516
Offal, clippings, &c	1.290
Lost	3.988
	100.000

In every 100 parts are contained—

	Water.	Ash.	Gluten.	Starch.
Groats and extra flour	10.6	0.41	11.7	70.0
Semmel or roll flour	10.5	0.60	13.3	67.2
Bread-flour	10.7	0.96	15.4	63.5
Black flour	9.5	1.55	14.9	61.0
Bran	10.7	5.46	14.3	43.6
Offal	9.2	2.65	15.2	0.0

Each 100 parts of flour contained—

Number.	Water.	Ash.	Nitrogen at 212°.	Nitrogen in common flour.	Starch.
A	11.050	0.398	2.089	1.858	69.983
B	11.545	0.386	1.874	1.658	69.530
0	11.077	0.380	2.010	1.808	72.145
1	10.618	0.416	2.071	1.851	71.017
2	10.492	0.452	2.087	1.868	68.867
3	10.142	0.481	2.122	1.907	68.386
4	10.421	0.586	2.212	1.981	67.302
5	10.544	0.611	2.435	2.178	67.176
6	10.748	0.764	2.611	2.329	65.631
7	10.674	1.176	2.788	2.491	61.773
8	9.527	1.549	2.570	2.325	61.031
9	10.690	5.240	2.518	2.249	45.838
10	11.150	5.680	2.513	2.233	41.453
11	9.235	2.648	2.616	2.375	0.000

In 100 parts of ash there are contained—

Number.	Fe_2O_3	CaO	MgO	KO	NaO	PO_5	Total.
A	0.525	7.296	6.899	34.663	0.988	49.721	100.092
B	0.583	7.718	6.857	34.669	0.891	49.218	99.936
0	0.630	8.057	7.008	35.482	0.744	48.976	100.125
1	0.643	7.946	7.105	35.285	0.675	48.976	100.428
2	0.627	7.454	7.795	34.254	0.678	49.519	100.327
3	0.635	7.094	8.343	33.876	0.690	49.306	100.344
4	0.596	6.798	9.924	32.715	0.650	50.056	100.739
5	0.570	6.791	10.574	32.239	0.726	50.187	100.087
6	0.334	6.626	10.870	30.386	0.946	50.146	99.308
7	0.425	5.536	12.234	30.314	1.260	50.204	99.973
8	0.484	4.741	12.947	30.299	0.974	50.173	99.618
9	0.208	2.747	16.861	30.672	0.701	50.152	101.341
10	0.436	2.502	17.349	30.142	1.080	49.112	101.621
11	1.671	8.203	13.023	31.489	2.144	44.054	100.584

The nitrogen gave of albuminoids—

(a, in normal flour; b, in normal flour, dried at 212° Fahrenheit,)

Number.	a	b	Number.	a	b
A	11.910	13.396	5	13.961	15.609
B	10.628	12.012	6	14.872	16.737
0	11.520	12.891	7	15.968	17.871
1	11.865	13.275	8	14.904	16.474
2	11.974	13.378	9	14.417	16.141
3	12.224	13.602	10	14.314	16.109
4	12.699	14.179	11	15.224	16.769

With the above numbers referred to 100 parts of whole wheat, the several percentages of milling products show the following composition:

Number.	Production.	Ash.	Nitrogen, a, 212°.	Nitrogen, b, normal flour.	a, albuminoids.	b, albuminoids.	Starch.
	Per cent.	Per cent.	Per cent.	Per cent.	Per cent.	Per cent.	Per cent.
A and B	0.489	0.0019	0.0096	0.0085	0.0629	0.0557	0.341
0	3.144	0.0121	0.0663	0.0596	0.4254	0.3824	2.268
1	2.635	0.0109	0.0545	0.0487	0.3498	0.3128	2.238
2	5.291	0.0239	0.1051	0.0940	0.6739	0.6028	3.543
3	7.165	0.0344	0.1520	0.1365	0.9744	0.8705	4.899
4	14.757	0.0864	0.3264	0.2923	2.0924	1.8744	9.931
5	17.925	0.1095	0.4364	0.3903	2.7979	2.5024	12.031
6	15.4195	0.1178	0.4025	0.3592	2.5807	2.3030	10.119
7	6.805	0.0800	0.1897	0.1694	1.2141	1.0867	4.203
8	2.576	0.0349	0.0662	0.0598	0.4245	0.3835	1.573
9	9.516	0.4886	0.2296	0.2139	1.5359	1.3712	4.261
10	9.000	0.5112	0.2261	0.2008	1.4427	1.2821	3.730
11	1.290	0.0341	0.0317	0.0287	0.2035	0.1842	
Total		1.4611	2.3066	2.0617	14.7781	13.2097	58.948
Found		1.505	2.503	2.2399	16.044	14.351	65.407
Difference		−0.044	−0.197	−0.178	−1.266	−1.142	−6.459

The proportions of the principal nutritive salts, as lime, magnesia, potassa and phosphoric acid, present themselves in the different products as follows:

Number.	Ca O	Mg O	K O	P O$_5$
A and B	0.00014	0.00013	0.00065	0.00090
0	0.00104	0.00085	0.00429	0.00595
1	0.00086	0.00077	0.00384	0.00531
2	0.00178	0.00186	0.00828	0.01183
3	0.00244	0.00287	0.01165	0.01696
4	0.00587	0.00857	0.02826	0.04325
5	0.00744	0.01158	0.03530	0.05495
6	0.00780	0.01280	0.03573	0.05972
7	0.00442	0.00978	0.02425	0.04016
8	0.00165	0.00452	0.01057	0.01851
9	0.01342	0.08238	0.15006	0.24505
10	0.01279	0.08865	0.15408	0.24106
11	0.00279	0.00444	0.01074	0.01502
Total	0.06584	0.22367	0.47897	0.75103
Found	0.06245	0.22920	0.47770	0.75887
Difference	+0.00339	−0.00553	+0.00127	−0.00784

According to this result there was lost—

Ash 0.043
Albuminoids 1.142
Starch 6.459
                                                                      ─────
                                                                      7.644

(3.988 of the product was dissipated; therefore, less than about 3.8 per cent. was found.)

The difference is to be sought in the starch, as the point where all the starch and dextrine are changed into sugar cannot be accurately determined.

The relations of phosphoric acid to nitrogen are as follows:

A and B .... 100 : 944
0 .... 100 : 1010
1 .... 100 : 911
2 .... 100 : 976
3 .... 100 : 807
4 .... 100 : 676
5 .... 100 : 710
6 .... 100 : 601
7 .... 100 : 422
8 .... 100 : 323
9 .... 100 : 87
10 .... 100 : 83
11 .... 100 : 191
12, (whole wheat) .... 100 : 295

These relations are graphically shown in the annexed diagram, Fig. 73.

Fig. 73.

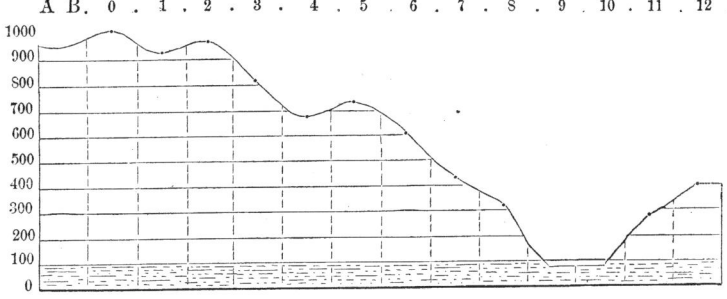

An analysis was made of a flour that contained all the bran, and it was found to be very nearly that of the whole kernel:

Water 10.743
Nitrogen 2.506
Starch 64.475
Ash, (containing Fe_2O_3, 0.852; CaO, 4.246; MgO, 14.721; KO, 31.898; NaO, 0.704; PO_5, 49.720 = 102.141) 1.503

Another flour, containing all the product except 13 per cent. of bran, was analyzed, and gave the following result:

Water	10.548
Nitrogen	2.518
Starch	65.660
Ash, (containing $Fe_2 O_3$, 1.338; Ca O, 5.085; Mg O, 12.425; K O, 31.456; Na O, 1.878; $P O_5$, 48.761 = 100.943)	1.032

These analyses show that the coarser the flour the more ash it contains, and the increase is proportioned to the increase of the lime and potassa and the diminution of the magnesia. The percentage of nitrogen increases to the bread-flour, Nos. 6 and 7, and diminishes with the bran, although the difference is only 0.8 per cent. (Dingler's Polytechnisches Journal, 1869, pp. 332–338; Annalen der Chemie und Pharmacie, 1869, Band cxlix, p. 343.)

APPENDIX B.

PHOSPHATIC BREAD.

233. IMPERFECTION OF THE VIENNA BREAD.—All improvements in making bread point to its being eaten fresh, but not warm. This necessity makes urgent the adoption of a process by which the labor of making the bread for household consumption shall be reduced to a minimum. Either the bread must be produced by a public baker, where the waiting-time can be utilized, or the yeast-process must, in private families, give place to a method which does not require the time and the care of this process, such as the process of self-raising flour.

With all its excellencies and attractiveness, the Vienna bread is not as nutritious as the rye-bread or as the brown wheat-bread.

The two most important nutritive constituents of the wheat are the albuminoid bodies, largely lodged in the gluten-coat of the grain, and the phosphates, which are associated with them. Both these constituents are largely lost from the flour both by the high and low milling processes. The percentage of nitrogen, which is the same in all the nitrogenous constituents of the wheat, is on an average not far from two, and deducting the weight of the woody fiber of the outer and inner coats of the bran, including the gluten-comb, but not the contents of the cells or the starch-granules embedded in it, which contain but little nitrogen, the nutritious portion of the berry contains *less* than two per cent. of nitrogen.

234. The flour of the great Pesth *Walzmühle* (cylinder-mill) at the Vienna Exposition yielded to my analyses the following percentages of nitrogen:

	Nitrogen.
Grits, A	2.25
No. 0	1.68
No. 1	1.68
No. 2	1.72
No. 3	1.72
No. 4	1.74
No. 5	1.80
No. 6	1.84
No. 7	1.80
No. 8	1.90
Bran, No. 9	1.98
Bran, No. 10	2.21

My analyses yielded also the following percentages of phosphoric acid:

	Phosphoric acid.
Grits, A	0.24
No. 0	0.14
No. 1	0.21
No. 2	0.22
No. 3	0.17
No. 4	0.25
No. 5	0.35
No. 6	0.24
No. 7	0.21
No. 8	0.36
Bran, No. 9	2.96
Bran, No. 10	1.74

The percentage of phosphoric acid in the whole grain is about one, (1.00.)

235. A glance at these results will show why the peasantry of Austria and Hungary, and, indeed, of Europe in general, prefer the black bread made from the whole meal, because of its greater nutritive value—because the laborer can be sustained on the black bread and cannot on the white. The consideration of these conditions led the late Baron Liebig to remark as follows:

"The significance of the nutritive salts in food is sufficiently well known to physiologists; it is known that without their co-operation the other constituents of the food are incapable of affording nourishment.

"By simple washing of fresh or boiled meat with water, which abstracts the nutritive salts, it would become incapable of serving in the preservation of life; the nutritive salts of wheat are identical with the nutritive salts of meat, and one understands that what is true for meat must also be true for bread, and that the nutritive value of flour is less in the same proportion as it contains less of the nutritive salts than the grain.

"The nutritive salts of meat and wheat are phosphates, and consist of compounds of phosphoric acid with potassa, lime, magnesia, and iron; the simple relations of the quantity of these substances, contained in wheat and flour, as shown by chemical analysis, will be sufficient to make obvious, the differences in the nutritive value of the two," &c.

236. The researches of Magendie, made many years since, established beyond question the superiority, for purposes of nutrition, of the bread made from whole meal as compared with bread made from the fine flour. He found that while dogs fed upon white wheat-bread alone after a time became ill, lost strength, and ultimately perished, dogs fed upon bread made from whole meal lived in health indefinitely long.

Chossat found that absolutely clean wheat—wheat that has been washed to remove any traces of calcareous earth adhering to its surface, would not sustain pigeons in health when supplied in addition with absolutely pure water only. After a time, their bones became thin and frail, and were unable to bear the weight of the birds; the phosphate of lime of the bones having been transferred to sustain the activity of organs more essential to life. They ultimately perished. Pigeons fed upon the same wheat and the same pure (distilled) water, and having access to lime compounds, continued in perfect health. Even pigeons nearly perished from having been fed only upon the diet first mentioned, upon being supplied with carbonate of lime were wholly restored to health.

237. It is well known that the peasantry, not of Austria only, but of all Europe, and a large proportion of the middle classes, habitually eat because of its nutritive value, brown bread; that is, a bread containing the bran with its phosphates. The higher classes in England prefer, two or three times a week, as an article of luxury, wheaten bread made from whole meal.

238. The nutritive value of oat-meal, and of the porridge made from oat-meal groats, an established dish upon the breakfast-table of Scotland, is well known.

The bread made from whole rye-meal, the *Pumpernickel* of Westphalia, containing all the phosphates due to the normal grain, is widely used by the best classes in Germany.

The rice, which is the great staple of food for so large a fraction of the oriental world, contains 20 per cent. more phosphoric acid in its ash and twice as much lime as the average wheat.

The Indian corn, the meal of which, wrought into the various forms of farinaceous food, has long been the basis of so large a proportion of the nutrition of the labor of the South in this country, differs but little in its percentage of phosphates from whole wheat.

239. These phosphates are indispensable to the nutrition of all higher organisms. They enter into, and constitute a part of, not only the bones, but every muscle, every nerve tissue; and in each secretory organ there seems to be a special accumulation, to be employed in the elaboration of the products which are secreted.

The observation that cattle prefer grass grown in meadows enriched with ground bone is in keeping with the practice, now well known, of feeding cattle upon bone-meal.

240. The significance of these considerations led to an investigation in Germany by M. Meyer of the effect of restoring in mineral condition the phosphates of rye-bran to the flour from which the bran had been separated. These experiments, made in 1870-'71, though less extended than might have been desired, and though defective somewhat in theory, so far as they went showed that, with the restoration of the phosphatic constituents of the bran, the bread was more nutritious than when made with the whole rye-meal including flour and bran.

241. The mode by which this restoration was effected consisted in the employment of an acid phosphate of lime and magnesia in the form of a dry powder; this was mixed with an alkaline carbonate sufficient to neutralize the acidity of the phosphoric acid, and these mixed powders intimately incorporated with the dry flour in such quantity as to restore to it the phosphoric acid, lime, magnesia, and alkali lost with the bran. On adding to this mixture of flour, acid phosphate, and alkaline carbonate, sufficient water or milk to produce with stirring a dough, the phosphoric acid and alkaline carbonate were dissolved, and reacting upon each other evolved carbonic acid in the form of gas. This gas appearing in every part of the dough gave it the required porosity or cellular structure, which was preserved by immediate baking.

242. The changes produced in the flour by this process are less than in the process of raising by yeast, partly because of the brief exposure of the gluten and starch to the solvent power of the water employed in making the dough, but chiefly because no deterioration of the nitrogenous constituents of the gluten or of the starch to supply material for the process of fermentation has taken place. The amount of the deterioration in nutritive value which bread made by the yeast or leaven process experiences, though doubtless frequently overestimated, is, nevertheless, considerable, even when pure press-yeast is employed, and much more when inferior yeast or old leaven is employed.

In the latter case, the deterioration is not confined to the degradation of the nitrogenous constituents and of the starch, yielding lactic, acetic, and other acids and offensive exhalations, but is seen in the imperfectly-raised, heavy, sodden, indigestible bread produced.

243. None of all this class of effects are produced in the process of raising with acid phosphate and a carbonated alkali. An excellence in the whitening of the crumb over that imparted to any bread produced by pure yeast, is to be ascribed to the action of the acid phosphate.

Another advantage in the phosphatic bread is that it contains no yeast-plants, and of course none to survive exposure to the heat of the baking temperature. As a consequence of the brief exposure to the action of water, the starch is less perfectly converted into the glassy texture, and is less liable to lose its cellular structure by pressure, and the walls, being coated with a larger proportion of granular starch, are less coherent. The crumb less easily loses its elasticity, less readily forms into compact boluses, and more readily imbibes the digestive fluids. As a consequence, persons of sensitive organs of digestion, who cannot eat hot yeast-bread, eat the hot phosphatic bread, enjoying the grateful aroma and flavor of fresh bread without conscious inconvenience. But the chief advantage is that to which Baron Liebig has called especial attention, the increase in the nutritive value, amounting to from 12 to 15 per cent., arising from the restoration of the phosphates lost with the bran. This bread having no yeast-plants does not mold, while great complaint was made of the

PHOSPHATIC BREAD. 113

army bread in use by the Austrian and German armies on account of its tendency to mold.

244. This mode of making bread, which was introduced by Baron Liebig into Germany, was tried in several kingdoms of Europe, and met with great acceptance in all particulars except one, and that was in the inferiority in size of the loaf produced from a given weight of flour with the phosphatic preparation as compared with the loaf produced by yeast.

As the phosphatic process has been successfully employed for a long period in the United States, and as the publications in relation to it have found their way into all the text-books, repertoriums, and recent chemical and industrial works, like "Enyrim on Baking," for example, and especially as Baron Liebig had taken much pains to introduce the method into Germany, it was natural that the inventor, although a juror, should be requested to exhibit the practical details of the process at the Exposition.

The Archduke Albrecht had remarked, in looking through the collections of improved arms and devices for the relief of the sick and wounded, that he saw nothing contemplating improvements in the food of the soldier in the field.

245. As the phosphatic method enables the soldier to provide himself with fresh bread equally nutritious, because containing all the phosphates of the original grain, and more nutritious, because more palatable, since it contains none of the objectionable peculiarities that attach themselves to the bread made with yeast or leaven from the whole meal; an offer was made by the inventor, "*hors concour*," as being a juror and commissioner, he could not be an exhibitor, to show the process in all its details to the war department of Austria. The offer was accepted, and the minister of war detailed a commission to witness the practical exhibition of the process at the Vienna bakery within the grounds of the Exposition. Through the kindness of Professor Schrötter, secretary of the Imperial Academy of Sciences, the conveniences of his laboratory at the imperial mint were placed at the disposal of the inventor for the preparation of the acid phosphate. With this acid powder and bicarbonate of soda, dough from the extra imperial flour, from rye-flour, and from a mixture of wheat and rye flour, was prepared in a few moments, and baked both in the oven and on the hearth outside, to show, in the interest of the military service, that the conveniences of the oven were not necessary in order to its ready baking.

In the latter experiment, the dough was placed between two thin sheet-iron troughs, (small stove-pipe cut in half lengthwise, and the straight edges flanged outward,) their curved surfaces turned toward each other encasing the dough, and the whole placed in hot ashes and coals. The exhibition was in all respects satisfactory. The loaves were

8 V B

porous in every part, and the taste in no respect inferior to the best Vienna bread made from corresponding flours. There were present at the exhibition of the process, besides the commission from the war department, Roman Uhl, who courteously placed the conveniences of the bakery at the disposal of the inventor, members of the international jury of the fourth group from various countries, and other gentlemen interested in the subject of improvements in the process of making bread.

246. It was obvious, as the result of this experiment, that by this process bread might be prepared at short notice from the Hungarian flour, which should unite all the excellencies of the Vienna bread made with press-yeast, and have restored to it all the nutritive value due to the phosphates of the original whole wheat.

247. REFERENCES.—In the preparation of the foregoing report, I have been indebted to various persons, whose names are given below, and who have aided me personally in the collection of material, or whose published researches and works I have consulted and quoted.

J. J. van den Wyngaert, Redacteur des wöchentlichen Journals "Die Mühle," 1872, 1873, and 1874.

Prof. Friederich Kick, "Mehlfabrikation," 1871, und "Officieller Bericht der Welt-Ausstellung, Gruppe IV, Sect. 1."

Prof. Carl Eugen Thiel und van den Wyngaert, "Officieller Bericht, Gruppe IV, Sect. 1."

Prof. Julius Wiesner, "Microscopische Untersuchungen," 1872, (Stuttgart.)

Dr. Wjatscheslaw Manassein, (St. Petersburg,) "Ueber die Beziehungen der Bacterien zum Penicillium glaucum u. s. w.," 1872.

Liebigs Annalen der Chemie und Pharmacie.

Wagner's Repertorium.

Comptes Rendus.

Enyrim, "Bäckergewerbe," Weimar, 1870.

Kerl und Stohmann's (Muspratt's) Technische Chemie.

Mitscherlich's Chemie.

Skizze der Landskunde Ungarns.

Thos. J. Hand, New York, "Wheat: its Worth and Waste," 1862.

Nature, 1870.

Prince Schwarzenberg; Heinrich Graf Zichy, President der IV ten Gruppe; Hofrath Dosswald; Dempwolff; Roman Uhl; Hassall; Pekar; von Fehling; von Bibra; Poggiale; Sachs; Laskowsky; Vogel; Alex. Muller; Oudemann; Mégé Mouriès; Reichenbach; Normandy; Heeren; Brefeld; Schrötter; Ritthausen; Thilenius; Mayer; Meyer; Jewell Bros.

INDEX.

	Article.	Page.
Acid, phosphoric—in ash	12	7
varies with nitrogen	39	15
tartaric, in self-raising flour	198	91
vegetable	19	9
Albumen, vegetable coagulation of—in baking	205	93
America, can we have Vienna bread in	226	102
American devices used in Austria	50	20
methods	137	65
wheat, impurities in	139	66
Analysis, table of	10	7
approximate	26	9
Dempwolff's	152	72
Apparatus, Paur's	69	32
required in the practice	81	36
Ash, distribution of material in the	11	7
phosphoric acid in the	12	7
constituents of the	13	8
proportions of	14	8
Australian wheat, result of harvesting Banat and	45	18
Austria, American devices used in	50	20
Bakers, method of London	196	90
Bakery, process in Vienna	217	97
phosphatic bread made at Vienna	243	112
Baking, coagulation of vegetable albumen in	205	93
Banat, result of harvesting and grinding—and Australian wheat	45	18
Barley-bread, why—is heavy	183	84
Beard, removal of	61	27
Berry, chemical composition of	9	6
proximate chemical ingredients of the	16	8
Bentz's method of removing beard and bran	61	27
Blondeau's view of yeast-cells	170	78
views of	176	80
Blows, effect of—on wheat	65	31
Bolt, the flour	109	49
Bolting or sifting	106	47
bran	78	35
Bran, composition of true	5	3
composition of inner layers of	6	3
illustration of structure of	7	3
removal of beard and	61	27
Bentz's method	61	27
duster	107	47
proportion of flour attached to	108	48
Bread, flour for Vienna	129	59
signification of the word	164	75

116 INDEX.

	Article.	Page.
Bread, leavened and unleavened	165	76
to secure porosity to the	166	77
why Hungarian flour will make light	183	84
why barley, rye, and oat is heavy	183	84
Paris wheat	193	88
Dauglish's aerated	199	91
phosphatic	200, 231	91
object of keeping—till it becomes stale	209	94
what is stale	210	94
advantages of Vienna	223	100
black—more nutritious	235	110
Meyer's experiment with phosphatic	238, 239	111
advantages of phosphatic	241	112
introduction of phosphatic—into Europe	242	112
phosphatic—made at the Vienna bakery	243	112
Brefeld's results of research upon alcoholic fermentation	181	83
Buchholz's cylinder-mills	132	61
Cake, leavened and unleavened	165	76
Caseine, vegetable fibrine and	21	9
Cells, necessity of preserving gluten	117	54
gluten—illustrated	146	69
size of starch—grains and gluten	154	73
size of yeast	169	78
Blondeau's views of yeast	170	78
cavities in yeast	172	79
effect of heat on	173	79
effect of solution of sugar on	173	79
having cavities convert sugar into alcohol and carbonic acid	175	80
Cerealine	24	9
Chemical composition of the berry	9	6
ingredients of the berry	16	8
constituents of gluten	31	12
examination of flour	161	75
Chossat, experiments of Magendie and	234	109
Climate, effect of—and other influences	27	10
nitrogen affected by	37	14
of Hungary	38	15
Color, redness of—in wheat	41	16
Congress of millers desirable	135	64
Cooling	95	42
indispensable in low milling	96	42
Corn, nutritive value of Indian	236	110
Crumb, test for phosphoric acid shows it everywhere in crust and	206	93
proportions of ingredients in	212	96
Crust, changes in the	203	92
test for phosphoric acid shows it everywhere in—and crumb	206	93
use of steam to prevent formation of thick	208	94
proportion of ingredients in	212	96
how to secure loaves of large size with thin	224	101
Cylinder-mill, the porcelain	102	44
Buchholz's	132	61
Cylinder-milling, methods of	97	42
illustration of	98	42
Dauglish's aerated bread	199	91

INDEX.

	Article.	Page.
Dempwolff's analysis	152	72
investigation of Hungarian wheat and wheat-flour from Pesth Walzmühle	229	103
Dextrine and sugar	20	9
and its homologues	32	13
conversion of starch to	203	92
Dirt, removal of	60	27
Diseases of wheat	51	21
Disintegrator, the	104	46
Dough, what causes it to "run"	160	74
action of lime-water in improving texture of	185	85
room	219	98
preparation of	220	99
how to make	227	103
Duster, the bran	107	47
Edges, effect of sharpness of cutting	80	36
European varieties	46	19
Fehling, loss of water as determined by	213	96
Ferment, what is a	178	82
substitutes for	197	90
Fermentation	167	77
theories of	177	81
alcoholic—dependent on dynamic conditions	180	83
effect of	182	83
loss due to	215	96
changes produced by—compared with those produced in the phosphatic process	240	111
Fibrine, vegetable—and caseine	21	9
Fife-wheat, Minnesota	122	56
process of milling	123	56
Flour, constitution and peculiarities of	79	36
bolt, the	109	49
for Vienna bread	129	59
southern	138	66
characteristics of	142, 150	67
Hungarian prize	149	71
composition of flour No. 0—and A grits	155	73
comparison of low and high milled	156	73
mode of testing	156	74
aroma of	159	74
chemical examination of	161	75
why Hungarian—will make light bread	183	84
tartaric acid in self-raising	198	91
changes of flour in becoming bread	201	92
Dempwolff's investigation of Hungarian wheat and wheat flour—from the Pesth Walzmühle	229	103
Horsford's analysis of prize—of Pesth Walzmühle	232	105
Gallen, St., mill	103	44
Gluten	17, 22	8
percentage in various flours	30	12
its chemical constitution	31	12
cells illustrated	146	69
size of—cells	154	73
changes of starch and	202	92

	Article.	Page.
Grades, proportion of—yielded by high and half-high milling	119	55
by numbers	127	59
made at Prague and other mills	130	60
Mège Mouriè's—of product of grinding	196	90
Grain, the several coatings of the	8	5
condition of phosphorus in the	33	13
character of Hungarian	42	16
separation of light	55	22
in the mill	93	41
structure of edible	147	69
effect of milling on the	148	70
Liebig's comparison of meats with	233	109
Grinding, result of harvesting and—Banat and Australian wheat	45	18
finer products of	76	35
Mège Mouriè's grades of product of	195	90
Grits, Vienna	67	31
unpurified	75	34
purification of	110	49
composition of 0 flour and A	155	73
nature and cause of	157	73
Groats of pumpernickel, nutritive value of	236	110
Grooves, arrangement of	85	37
use of the	86	38
various forms of the	89	40
dimensions adopted	91	40
Harvesting, result of—and grinding Banat and Hungarian wheat	45	18
Hassall, views of	176	80
Heat, effect on cells	173	79
Heating	88	39
prevention of	48	20
Horsford, experimental researches, result of	211	95
analysis of prize flour of Pesth Walzmühle	232	105
Hungarian wheat	36	14
comparison of Victoria with—wheat	40	15
character of—grain	42	16
tables of varieties of—wheat	43	16
hardiness of—wheat	64	30
products of—high milling	125	57
details of—milling process	126	57
mills, average product of	133	61
prize flour	149	71
mill industry	163	75
why—flour will make light bread	183	84
Dempwolff's investigation of—wheat and wheat-flour from Pesth Walzmühle	229	103
Hungary, climate of	38	15
Impurities of wheat	52	21
in American wheat	139	66
Indian corn, nutritive value of	236	110
Ingredients, source of mineral—of flour	15	8
proximate chemical—of the berry	16	8
in crust and crumb, proportion of	212	96
Jewell Brothers' practice	141	67
Jury classification	71	33
comparison by international	128	59

INDEX.

	Article.	Page.
Kaiser-semmel	1, 218	1
illustrations of	222	100
Lands, arrangement of—and grooves	85	37
Liebig's views	179	82
Manassein supports	179	82
comparison of meats with grain	233	109
Lime-water, action of—in improving texture of dough	185	85
Loaves, advantage to consumers of rolls rather than	225	102
Machines, smut	62	28
Magendie, experiments of	234	109
Manassein supports Liebig's views	179	82
Mautner, press-yeast of	187	86
Method of thrashing	49	20
Bentz's—of removing beard and bran	61	27
older—of milling	66	31
Ignaz Paur's—of milling	68	32
American	137	65
London bakers'	196	90
Meyer's experiments with phosphatic bread	238, 239	111
Middlings or unpurified grits	75	34
Mill, grain in the	93	41
porcelain cylinder	102	44
Saint Gallen	103	44
grades made at Prague and other	130	60
products of the Prague	131	60
Buchholz cylinder	132	61
average product of the Hungarian	133	61
Hungarian—industry	163	75
Millers, a congress of—desirable	135	64
Milling, older methods of	66	31
origin of high	67	31
difference between high and low	70	32
detailed description of high	72	33
character of high	74	34
products of low	77	35
cooling indispensable in low	96	42
method of cylinder	97	42
illustration of cylinder	98	42
advantages of cylinder	100	44
advantages of high	116	54
half-high	118	55
process of low	120	55
process of "Fife" wheat	123	56
high	124	56
products of Hungarian high	125	57
details of Hungarian process	126	57
products of low	134	63
effect of—on grains	148	70
products of	230	104
Millstones	82	36
the Thilenius	92	40
Minnesota "Fife" wheat	122	56
Mitscherlich's observations on growth of yeast-plant	171	78

INDEX.

	Article.	Page.
Mourié's, Mège, method	194	89
grading of products of grinding	195	90
Nitrogen; its proportion affected by climate	37	14
phosphoric acid varies with	39	15
distribution of	151	71
Oats, removal of	54	22
why rye—and barley bread is heavy	183	84
meal-porridge, nutritive value of	236	110
Oil	23	9
Paris wheat-bread	193	88
Pasteur, his views	176	80
different yeast-plants required for different products	179	82
Pastry, leavened and unleavened	165	76
Paur's, Ignaz, method of milling	68	32
apparatus	69	32
purifier	111	50
Pesth, purifier used at	112	50
Pesth Walzmühle, Dempwolff's investigation of Hungarian wheat and wheat flour from the	229	103
Pesth Walzmühle, Horsford's analysis of prize flour of	232	105
Phosphates and sulphates	29	12
indispensable to vital tissue	237	111
Phosphatic bread	200, 231	91
Meyer's experiment with—bread	238, 239	111
changes produced by fermentation compared with those produced in the—process	240	111
advantages of—bread	241	112
Phosphatic bread introduction into Europe	242	112
made at Vienna bakery	243	112
Phosphoric acid varies with nitrogen	39	15
test for, shows it everywhere in crust and crumb	206	93
Phosphorus, condition of—in the grain	33	13
Pile, what is it?	214	96
Plant, structure of the	47	19
Porridge, nutritive value of oatmeal	236	110
Porcelain cylinder-mill	102	44
Prague, grades made at—and other mills	130	60
mill, product of	131	60
Pressed-yeast, the	187	86
production from 1846 to 1872	188	86
preparation of	189	87
Pressure, effect of blows and—on the grain	65	31
Products, grades of	73	34
Pumpernickel of Westphalia	192	88
nutritive value of groats of	236	110
Purification	121, 140	55
Purifier used at Pesth	112	50
Report, scope of the	3	2
Research, result of Horsford's experiments	211	95
Rice of Indian corn, nutritive value of	236	110
Rolls, advantage to consumers of—rather than bread	225	102
Rye, why oat—and barley bread is heavy	183	84
Scourer	63	29
Seeds, separating round	56	24
separating and winnowing	53	22
Sifting and bolting	106	47

INDEX.

	Article.	Page.
Smut-machine	62	28
Southern flour	138	66
Starch	18	9
character of various—granules	145	68
grains, size of	154	73
changes of—and gluten	202	92
conversion of—to dextrine	203	92
Steam, uses of—to prevent formation of thick crust	208	94
Structure of the granule	144	68
of edible grains	147	69
Sugar and dextrine	20	9
Sulphates and phosphates	29	12
Tartaric acid in self-raising flour	198	91
Thilenius millstone, the	92	40
United States, form of grooves used in	87	37
Vegetable albumen	19	9
fibrine and caseine	21	9
Ventilation	94	42
Victorian, comparison of—with Hungarian wheat	40	15
Vienna bread, manufacture of	2	1
grits	67	31
flour for—bread	129	59
bakery processes	217	97
advantages of—bread	223	100
can we have—bread in America	226	102
bakery, phosphatic bread made at the	243	112
Water	25	9
action of lime—in improving texture of dough	185	85
loss of—as determined by von Fehling	213	96
Walzmühle, Wegmann's	101	44
Pesth, Dempwolff's investigation of Hungarian wheat and wheat-flour from	229	103
Horsford's analysis of prize flour from Pesth	232	105
Wegmann's Walzmühle	101	47
Westphalian pumpernickel	192	68
Wheat, description of the grain of	4	2
Hungarian	36	14
comparison of Victorian with Hungarian	40	16
redness of color in; its causes	41	16
table of varieties of Hungarian	43	16
kinds generally sown	44	18
European varieties	46	19
diseases and enemies of	51	21
Minnesota "Fife"	122	56
Paris—bread	193	88
Dempwolff's investigation of Hungarian—and—flour from Pesth Walzmühle	229	103
Winnowing and separating	53	22
Wiesner's views of yeast-plant	176	82
Yeast-bread, problem of a	186	86
cell, size of a	169	78
Blondeau's view of the	170	78
cavities of the	172	79

	Article.	Page.
Yeast-plant, the	168	77
Mitscherlich's observations on growth of	171	78
illustration of growth of	175	80
different—requires different products	179	82
pressed	187	86
production of—from 1846 to 1872	188	86
preparation of	189	87
Zettler's mode of preparation of pressed yeast	190	87

Printed in Poland
by Amazon Fulfillment
Poland Sp. z o.o., Wrocław

68552971R00074